socialsklz :-) ™
FOR SUCCESS

socialsklz :-)™

FOR SUCCESS

HOW TO GIVE CHILDREN THE SKILLS THEY NEED TO THRIVE IN THE MODERN WORLD

FAYE DE MUYSHONDT

RUNNING PRESS
PHILADELPHIA · LONDON

Books published by Running Press are available at special discounts for bulk purchases in the United States by corporations, institutions, and other organizations. For more information, please contact the Special Markets Department at the Perseus Books Group,
2300 Chestnut Street, Suite 200, Philadelphia, PA 19103,
or call (800) 810-4145, ext. 5000,
or e-mail special.markets@perseusbooks.com.

ISBN 978-0-7624-4932-3

Library of Congress Control Number: 2013932803
E-book ISBN 978-0-7624-4934-7

9   8   7   6   5   4   3   2   1
Digit on the right indicates the number of this printing

Cover and interior design by Bill Jones
Edited by Kristen Green Wiewora
Illustrations by Shaw Nielsen
Typography: Myriad and Officina Serif

Running Press Book Publishers
2300 Chestnut Street
Philadelphia, PA 19103-4371

Visit us on the web!
www.runningpress.com

This book is dedicated to my parents,
Anne and Ed Rogaski,
who instilled in me the many skills
that I am now blessed to teach.
I love you, Mom and Dad.

Table of Contents

Acknowledgments

Thank you to the many, many students I've been fortunate to work with, who have given me so much joy and made my "business" world so fulfilling.

Thank you Jennifer Kasius, who believed in this book and made a dream come true.

I'm so grateful to Monique Owens, my colleague, who helped me during long days at the office of brainstorming, writing, re-writing, editing, and helping decipher my random thoughts out loud into something that actually made sense on paper.

An enormous thanks to my spectacular editor, Kristen Green Wiewora who worked her magic on this book when it was desperately needed, who patiently held my hand as I embarked on this brand-new experience and who offered empathy as I worked through the "drudgery" of the editing process! Special thanks to August Tarrier and Victoria Fiengo.

And my very, very dear friend Chaz Ross who not only encouraged me to start social-sklz:-) some years ago, but who has been my confidant in everything since then.

Thank you Gillian Berman who has become that much more special as a friend because of this book.

Thank you Tom and Harland Dahl who listened and gave nuggets of wisdom throughout this journey!

Thank you my precious baby Adriana Elizabeth, at whom I gazed at in amazement as I wrote this book.

And thank you to the love of my life, Federico, who fuels me each day with the love, guidance, and support that I need to thrive in my modern world.

Introduction

The idea for teaching modern day social skills and eventually launching my business, socialsklz:-) tools to thrive in the modern world, came to me about six years ago. I'd spent 15 years in public relations and marketing, building brands, garnering media attention, and managing reputations. As part of that work, I also offered media training for clients to get them ready for print interviews, national TV, and radio. In this training, we'd thoroughly review verbal and non-verbal first impressions, including body language, speaking, intonation, responding to questions, appearance, and such. During those media training sessions I'd often think of how valuable those lessons could be to anyone. But for many of us, these lessons were anything but a positive learning experience: what we got were critical comments from a family member, chiding us for our behavior.

In 2007, I began teaching at New York University in the Steinhardt School of Media, Culture, and Communications; in teaching PR 101, I was reminded of my media training sessions and realized that my students were in dire need of them. When they gave presentations, it was common to hear frequent use of "like, "um," and "ya know," and they didn't seem to think it was a problem to be standing in front of the class with their midriffs showing. As part of their coursework, students would "friend" me on Facebook for a ten-day period to keep me abreast of the social media work they were doing for class, but when I logged in I was more likely to find various students' salacious photos and racy status updates in my newsfeed.

Students would make a request by email without bothering to use a greeting, address me properly, or even close with a "thank you." They spent class time staring at their computer screens, so it was nearly impossible for many to make eye contact during discussions, and the few who did seemed like anomalies. As the economy plummeted, those same students complained about how frustrating the job market was and how difficult it was to secure a job. Rather than mutter under my breath "these kids today," I started to ponder the truly valuable skills, entirely outside of academics, that help to win a job interview, particularly when the competition is fierce. And while grades and, yes, perhaps a good school, are vitally important, I realized that that would only get their resume in the door for an interview. The real clincher would be excellent social interaction and communication skills—essentially, their social IQ.

With the rise of modern technology, it's clear that face-to-face interaction seems less important to upcoming generations. More and more, young people are communicating via email, text, and even social media. However, it's clearer than ever just how important social skills are, not only for an interview, but for life. It's what compelled me to develop a course for college students in which they learn essential social skills, appropriately titled "The Brand Called You."

The course addresses topics such as first impressions, body language, conversational skills, grooming, the overuse of filler words (like, um, and ya know), greetings and introductions, appropriate attire for business and non-business encounters, technology dos and don'ts, respect for oneself and others, digital responsibility, showing and expressing gratitude, and the importance of taking ownership and pride in what one does. At the end of the class, the students give a 30-second "elevator speech" about themselves—in other words, a pitch deliverable in the time span of an elevator ride, a maximum of 30 seconds and 140 words, or in more modern terms, an "elevator tweet."

Teaching "The Brand Called You" showed me how empowering these skills are for college students, and I quickly realized that we should be teaching social interaction and communication skills, like any other important subject, rather than assuming that those skills would be acquired passively through daily social interaction. For most people, good social skills aren't an inherent character trait, but the good news is that, just like any other skill set, they can be mastered over time, if they're taught, practiced, and implemented. I see this firsthand in the classroom—and the younger the learner, the better.

Tara Parker Pope's *New York Times* article titled "School Curriculum Falls Short on Bigger Lessons"[1] brought the issue to readers' attention:

Now that children are back in the classroom, are they really learning the lessons that will help them succeed? Many child development experts worry that the answer may be 'no.' They say the ever-growing emphasis on academic performance and test scores means many children aren't developing life skills like self-control, motivation, focus, and resilience, which are far better predictors of long-term success than high grades. And it may be distorting their and their parents' values.

I decided to try out "The Brand Called You" with a younger age set, and began volunteer-teaching a modified version to students from New York public schools, including PS 140, AGL, and Booker T. Washington, in addition to organizations, including the YMCA, Big Brothers Big Sisters, and Girl Scouts of America. I wasn't interested in holding Old World manners and etiquette classes that featured white gloves and pinkies held up at high tea, so I began teaching the same interactive workshops for the real world that I conducted at NYU. With age-appropriate modifications, I taught the importance of making a good first impression, respect and consideration, greetings and introductions, initiating and maintaining conversations, and online reputation management. With the younger set, I focused more on eye contact, body language, positive behavior, and listening and respect.

What became evident at these workshops was how empowering these skills were for children; the fact that they were learning in a fun, interactive setting resulted in an incredible success rate. Although they only want the best for their children, parents tend to address or teach good social skills in a corrective mode. That is, rather than couch the lessons as a learning opportunity, like science, tennis, ballet, or any other activity, parents tend to assume kids pick up these skills on their own. And then, when kids are out in public, parents have a tendency to correct them for things they haven't learned: "Why didn't you say 'hello'?" and, "Look Mrs. Smith in the eye."

After one parent/child program, I got a note from a parent, Carolyn: "This was so much fun and so clever. It is so difficult to teach children/teens manners without them feeling criticized and judged by us. This concept works. The message is learned without you forcing it." And from another parent, Audrey: "The boys were absolutely buzzing when they left class, you really gave them a lot to think about and practice. We are particularly pleased with the retention of the information from class—you have developed great pedagogical frames for each area, and as I suspected, this environment is far superior to my husband and I lecturing at home."

I could see firsthand how meaningful and effective the classes were, and I made sure to offer up the lessons in a proactive and fun mode. Through these classes, children as young as four years old begin to open up socially, gaining confidence and self-esteem. Parents like Carolyn and Audrey see the impact that the classes have, not to mention how enthusiastic their children are about the program and how anxious they are to return to class. Notes like the ones above compelled me to make the classes available to the general public. In October 2009, I held the very first *socialsklz:-) tools to thrive in the modern world* workshop in the conference room of my public relations office in New York City.

Dr. Barbara Howard, an assistant professor of pediatrics at the Johns Hopkins School of Medicine and an expert on behavior and development, explains that a child's social skills should be measured during an annual check-up: "Social skills are necessary for school success; they affect how you do on the playground, in the classroom, [and] in the workplace."[2] I could not agree more. In a world where kids are so programmed and scheduled, when they're taking part in countless activities and sports, what matters most is how they apply those skills in a social setting. The earlier we begin instilling these lessons, the more empowered and self-confident children will be, and the more equipped they will be to have a successful and fruitful life.

Dr. Kenneth Ginsburg, an expert in adolescent medicine at the Children's Hospital of Philadelphia, poses the question, "What are we really trying to do when we think about raising kids?" And he explains, "We're trying to put in place the ingredients so the child is going to be a successful 35-year-old. It's not really about getting an A in algebra."[3] While formal education is important, in my opinion, teaching children how to interact socially with others is more important.

Over the course of teaching, I've found many valuable studies that back up what happens in the classroom. A comprehensive analysis of 33 studies by a team of scientists at Loyola University, Chicago, compared traditional academic study with social and emotional learning (SEL) programs that required child learners to be interactive and to react to and process emotion through role-playing and other social themes. It turned out that children learned better when they had access to SEL programs. The analysis claimed that "teaching kids social and emotional skills leads to an average 11 percentile-point gain in their academic performance over six months compared to students who didn't receive that same instruction."[4] In his *New York Times* best-selling book *How Children Succeed*, Paul Tough argues that high scores on SATs and academic performance may not necessarily be what matters most; it is instead a child's character that matters.[5]

I have worked with children, teens, and young adults over the years, including a 25-year-old who had gone to an excellent school and had great SAT scores, yet wasn't able to land a job after graduating. His mom reached out via email with the subject line "HELP!" confessing that she and her husband were the stereotypical helicopter parents who wanted the very best for their son and had perhaps done too much for him. In hindsight, she saw that in making so many decisions for him, she had not allowed him to learn the necessary social and communications skills for himself, and so her son was struggling in his interactions with others. This guidebook will provide the lessons to teach your child skills that will help in functioning as an adult.

SETTING THE RECORD STRAIGHT

I want to set the record straight. I'm not Emily Post, nor am I striving to be the Amy Vanderbilt of the technology era. I am neither a "manners maven," nor a self-appointed etiquette expert. I cringe when I am introduced at a cocktail party as the "etiquette guru"—people stand up straighter, button up, and get nervous. I watch them second-guess their handshakes and stumble through "eloquent" introductions of themselves as they struggle to remember whether they said, "It's nice to meet you, too." I am not that woman.

The foundation of the socialsklz:-) program wasn't to teach manners and etiquette, although some of the lessons might fall into that category. I developed it to instill the vital life skills that are often not taught in schools, but that set up our children for success. My goal in creating the programs that now make up socialsklz:-) was simply to guide children by teaching them the social and emotional tools they will use every day for the rest of their lives. When you purchase this book, you're taking a proactive stance toward ensuring that your child will be a socially well-adapted adult.

There is no question in my mind that social skills are the single most important lesson you can teach your children; they are the foundation for everything they will do. Starting with that first "Mommy & Me" class, to the first play date, the first day of kindergarten or college, and throughout life, social skills are invaluable. We've all seen someone walk into the room smiling, head held high, exuding confidence and charisma, and thought to ourselves: "Wow, she has presence," or, "That's someone I want to meet." You often hear that a successful job interview can be determined in the first 5 minutes. Wouldn't you want your child to grow up to be that grown-up?

But just what are "social skills?" Is it nothing more than the media buzzword du jour? Are social skills exclusively for kids with special needs? Absolutely not. Unlike traditional manners and etiquette, these are the tools needed to build confidence, solve problems, and navigate through life. In this book you'll find exercises that lay the foundation for acquiring a winning set of social skills which will help children excel in the modern world—and even stand out.

We have classes for tennis, art, soccer, ballet, piano, martial arts, cooking and every extracurricular activity, even though most children will never go on to use these skills past their high school years. But social interaction and communication skills are used for life—starting in childhood and through adolescence into adulthood—and yet they aren't offered as extracurricular lessons. Your kids will use these skills *forever,* and if they are carefully honed, just like any other skill set, they will undoubtedly make your children's lives more rewarding and fulfilling.

Most schools now are grappling with budget cuts and overcrowded classrooms, and so they are unable to emphasize social and emotional intelligence. And that means that the onus is on parents and caregivers. Have you ever sat down with your children and taught them how to make a good first impression or give a proper handshake? Typically, parents think that kids will acquire these skills through social interaction, or they believe that if they correct their kids they will learn good social skills. In reality, these skills need to be actively taught and practiced regularly, just like any sport or instrument.

You may be thinking that these sorts of skills don't come naturally to your child. That's okay. Good social interaction and communication skills are not instinctual for many kids, but when you teach these skills, and the instruction is accompanied by repetition and practice, they can become a natural part of children's everyday lives. I've been teaching this program for the past six years, and I see firsthand that these skills can indeed be learned, especially if you present them in a pleasant interactive setting. Helen Kramer, an expert in emotional education, explains, "We now know that our brains are plastic and are capable of learning new patterns throughout the course of our lives. We also know that 'nurture' trumps 'nature' and that if we are not born with skills we can learn them if we are taught in a supportive environment. No matter what our genetic predispositions, through repetition we can create new neural pathways creating new thoughts, feelings and behaviors."[6]

This book will give you the tools to instill these lessons at home. The beauty of teaching at home is that you'll have the opportunity to practice a great deal. And when you first see your children confidently introducing themselves and making eye contact, or when a teacher comments on your child's respectfulness, not only will you be proud, you will also see your child's newfound sense of self-esteem. After our workshops, many parents tell me they receive compliments from others on how polite or engaging their child is.

WHY THIS BOOK?

It is no secret that these days many Americans believe respect and courtesy to be in short supply. The Public Agenda released a study entitled, "Land of the Rude: Americans in New Survey Say Lack of Respect is Getting Worse," stating that, "Seventy-nine percent of Americans say the lack of respect and courtesy should be regarded as a serious national problem."[7] *The New York Times* featured an article by Christine Pearson, "Use of Tech Devices Harm Workplace

Relationships," which highlights the fact that technological devices have led to a greater degree of incivility.[8] In *The Best Advice I Ever Got*, Katie Couric quotes actress Nia Vardalos, who explained that the best advice she ever got was to be polite. She advised that you need to learn to rise above challenges, and claims that the only thing you can do when you encounter rudeness is to respond with politeness.

Each day, we're faced with a barrage of technology, and this barrage diminishes the amount of face-to-face interaction we engage in. It's not just this generation of young people: it's every upcoming generation too, as technology will continue to play a larger and larger role. My suggestion? Embrace it, just as kids do, but at the same time, know that it's even more crucial to teach good social interaction and communication skills. And it's up to us to do the teaching.

Although socialsklz:-) workshops are sometimes categorized as "manners" and "etiquette" classes, you'll note that I don't use these words when I describe the program. Although I did go to an etiquette school to get certified to teach proper dining, I quickly realized that I only wanted dining to be a part of what I taught. My real focus was on social IQ, including topics such as shaking hands and making a good first impression, and thoughtfulness and empathy.

To that end, children cringe at the words "etiquette" and "manners." When they're told that they have to attend a "manners" class, they walk in angry. This became strikingly evident when I overheard a student in a socialteenz class say to her peer, "My mom told me these were manners classes, but they're so much more fun than that." Parents often call to say that while their children would really benefit from these classes, they didn't know how to get their kids to attend. Let's face it: we live in a casual society in which Old World manners and etiquette don't strike a chord in children. For this reason, the way parents market the workshops to their children is crucial. I urge parents to tell their kids that these are "life skills" classes that will help them be their best selves and that will make life easier and more fun. I kick off workshops by asking kids why they think they're in the classroom: some say that they're there for "manners," some don't say anything because they think their parents have done them a great disservice in sending them, and then there are a few youngsters who excitedly raise their hands and say that they've come for "princess" classes. I then pose the questions: "Do you want to have an easier life? Do you want to hear 'yes' more than 'no'? Do you want to be the best person you have the power to be?" to which all the students respond enthusiastically. And while we may not have fairytale princes and princesses walking out of our workshops, we do have kids who are more socially adept and very eager to return for more lessons.

Simply put, the words "manners" and "etiquette" have a staid, outdated association that is a far cry from the fast-paced world our kids live in today.

These are digital citizens who have a voice and who are living in a world where everyone is accessible, or at least approachable, via the Internet. These are kids who have more rights and more of a say in their own lives than ever before. And this is a world in which, according to a Pew Research Study, the average teen sends over 50 text messages a day, and a country in which many prominent figures, and even our President, are accessible via social networking sites.[9]

Through the socialsklz:-) program, I've seen what works and what sticks with children, tweens, and teens. Kids and parents alike compel me to develop more programs and expand because they want to return for more workshops. They also write letters proclaiming, "My son has never made eye contact before in his life, and now he does!" and "My child loved class and is so excited to return to work on his first impression." These letters, among many others, prove just how valuable the classes have been. There is no question that these skills are empowering and rewarding for children. I have been empowered as well, and I hope you will be too. There is no greater gift than instilling self-confidence and self-esteem in children by teaching and equipping them with a social and emotional toolkit for life.

Stephanie Ogozalek of Mommy Poppins® says of the program: "The overall message of the program is respect for yourself and others, and since the class we have witnessed the most amazing behavior shift in my son. He is listening to us and in turn his behavior has improved. And at this workshop he learned it was 'bad manners' to have people say something to you more than once. A total breakthrough for my boy."

❦ HOW TO USE THIS BOOK ❧

As a result of the local and national media coverage that socialsklz:-) has garnered, I often get phone calls and emails from people around the country, and even outside the US, asking when we're coming to their towns. Although it's been my dream to rent a big school bus and go on a socialsklz:-) tour of America, for the moment, this book is my way of reaching out to all of you at home who can't take the subway up to West 85th Street here in New York City.

I commend you for recognizing the need for these skills to be taught, buying the book, and setting out to instill these lifelong lessons. While the workshop format, where kids are taught by people other than their parents and participate with other kids, has its advantages, the big advantage you have in teaching this skill set at home is that you can work on reinforcing it day by day. This book is meant to aid you, the parent, in incorporating social skills into your children's lives without being perceived as a "nag" or a "critic." The method we use is tried and true, and it works. I'd suggest doing a chapter a week for a ten-week period. The time in between lessons will allow you to put the newly learned skills to use in your daily routine.

Each chapter is divided into three sections: interactive Lesson, Review and

Practice, and Application and Goals. This three-pronged style of teaching is one that I've used over and over, and it has proven to be tremendously effective and enjoyable. Another idea is to make this your own "socialsklz:-) project" and invite your child's friends and their parents to partake as well. Each household can host various lessons, and you can stay involved with other families by reading this book together. I'd also suggest that you and each of your children keep special journals as you progress through the book; the journals make a great supplement to the lessons and you'll have an opportunity to refer back to them, as many of the chapters encompass previous lessons. You can download your very own free socialsklz:-) journal on our website at www.socialsklz.com. The downloadable journals are similar to the ones I use when I work privately with children and their parents. As you proceed through the book, you'll see suggestions for various journal entries, and feel free to add more as you see fit.

I designed the journal to be a fun accompaniment to the lessons, rather than something that becomes a chore. For this same reason, I decided not to include a socialsklz:-) workbook to accompany the workshops because I wanted to make sure we emphasized the "fun" factor.

One reason that we've had such success is that kids don't feel as if they're "in school." As MommyPoppins.com said, we're "not your mother's manners classes." When kids arrive, music is playing, we have an "adult" conference table, and we teach the lessons in a way that kids relate to and want to apply to their lives. We practice what they've learned, using repetition, and then we immediately put their new skills to use in a real world setting. That's precisely what this book will show you how to do—and you may learn a thing or two along the way! Parents often tell me that even years after their children have completed the workshops, their kids are still correcting them at the dinner table. So beware, you might end up with your very own socialsklz:-) violations squad on your hands!

I very much look forward to working with you (and your children). Should you have any questions along your journey, feel free to reach out to me by email at faye@socialsklz.com.

1

Face to Face: Making a Good First Impression

*"First impressions are more heavily influenced
by nonverbal cues than verbal cues.
In fact, studies have found that nonverbal cues
have over four times the impact
on the impression you make than
anything you say."*[1]

—Dr. Carol Kinsey Goman,

President of Kinsey Consulting Services

We have all heard the warning, "You never get a second chance to make a good first impression," and if you think about it, it is true. How many times have you referred back to that first impression that someone had of you? So what exactly is a first impression? What goes into making a first impression? How long does it take to make one?

Your children will be making first impressions throughout their lives: through kindergarten, high school, camp, college, the workplace . . . they will always be making first impressions. A first impression is how you come across to others—essentially, how you represent yourself every day. At New York University, I always told my students that "you are your own brand" and that "you have choices about how you manage that brand each day." Without saying a word, the subconscious mind evaluates a person in seconds and then looks for characteristics to validate that first impression. Researchers say it takes 3 to 7 seconds to make a first impression of someone or something. It's not fair, but it's also a fact. During one of my workshops, a student countered, "I thought you should never judge a book by the cover." Although it's an unjust reality, I explained that it is human nature to make a quick assessment of someone. And because that is the case, why wouldn't we want to make good first impressions if it is in our power to do so?

Princeton University psychologist Alex Todorov and co-author Janine

Willis, a student researcher who graduated from Princeton in 2005, had people look at a microsecond of video footage of two political candidates. What's fascinating is that people could predict with 70-percent accuracy who would win the election just from that microsecond of tape.

This tells us that people can make incredibly accurate snap judgments in a fraction of a second.

Another example is the often-discussed first televised presidential debate, in 1960, between Richard Nixon and John F. Kennedy. Kennedy arrived for the debates from Florida looking tan and well-rested, while Nixon was recovering from a knee injury he suffered during the contentious campaign. Kennedy came across as telegenic, calm, and comfortable in front of the cameras, but Nixon appeared nervous and sweaty, his five o'clock shadow all-too-obvious under the bright lights. Radio listeners of the first debate narrowly awarded Nixon a victory, while the larger television audience believed Kennedy won by a wide margin.

Since each of us makes a first impression day in and day out for a lifetime, doesn't it make sense to teach our kids how to make a winning first impression? We inherently know the value of a first impression; if our children can make a good first impression, it will open many doors—at school, with teachers, in making friends, meeting others, and later in all aspects of life. Among the myriad emails I've received from parents and students over the years, this one from Tanya Hill still makes me smile: "Last Sunday at church, my daughter met someone new. She smiled, gave a firm handshake, and confidently looked that person in the eye. I was not around, but a friend called me the next day. My daughter loved the class and really wants to continue after the four-session workshop. I expect that she will be a repeat customer. Keep up the good work."

For some kids, making a good first impression is easy and comes naturally, but for most, it doesn't. Because it is rare to inherently know how to make a good first impression, I can easily recall each of my students who had that quality. There are many components that go into making a good first impression and they all work together—you can't isolate just one and hope to come across in a positive way. This lesson is so important but it isn't taught anywhere else in a child's life, so really take the time to work through this lesson and practice, practice, practice.

FIVE COMMON PROBLEMS CHILDREN HAVE WITH FACE-TO FACE INTRODUCTIONS

• They don't make eye contact

• Their body language is poor

• They don't speak clearly or at all

• They don't introduce themselves

• They don't convey warmth or they don't smile

LESSON

By the end of this chapter, your children should be able grasp the key aspects of a good first impression, how to properly greet others, and how to introduce themselves to new adults and peers with confidence.

*Before you get started with the lesson, either download our free social-sklz:-) journal from our website, www.socialsklz.com, or have your own journal ready to make the first entry.

❧ YOUR FIRST IMPRESSION ☙

Explain to your kids that you're going to make two first impressions and that they're going to need to write down a few things about each and then compare first impression A to first impression B. This will serve as their very first journal entry, which they can title "First Impressions" or whatever creative title you come up with.

As you walk into the room to make each of the two distinct first impressions, you won't speak at all. Be sure that you actually walk out of the room and pause before entering for each impression. For first impression A, demonstrate the following behavior:

- **Keep your eyes on the floor, only occasionally glancing up**
- **Nervously twirl your hair or play with the hem of your shirt**
- **Slouch your shoulders**

- Suddenly move to the table and anxiously take a seat without pulling out the chair completely
- Sit sideways, with your elbows on the table and your hand resting on your chin

Ask children to write out a few characteristics of entrance A. For the younger age set, give a few examples of descriptive words: "happy, sad, nervous." There will undoubtedly be a few laughs. If children need further encouragement, ask if they thought that person was nice, warm, shy, or friendly. As soon as the exercise is complete, ask kids to put their pens down.

Explain that you're now going to make first impression B and that they need to similarly dissect this next first impression. Walk back out of the room, pause, and reenter. During first impression B, display the following behavior:

- SMILE!
- Stand up straight
- Make eye contact with each person in your presence
- Keep your hands at your sides as you walk in energetically
- Take a seat by pulling out your chair and sitting properly at the table, keep smiling

Once children are through with their first impressions of entrance B, go over their responses. Point out that neither person A nor person B said a thing, and that each person took only about 10 seconds to come in and take his or her seat. In a brief period and with no conversation, your kids were able to draw a number of conclusions about that person. I often get words like "happy, nice, friendly, kind" in response to impression B.

Ask the following questions: Which of those people would you like to meet and make friends with? Which person would you like to sit next to? Which first impression would you prefer to make?

After the first impression exercise, some parents have raised a concern about shyness. If your child is shy, will he or she be able to make a good impression? I've had a number of very shy students over the years and I want to be clear that I often see children overcoming shyness. Teaching social interaction and communication skills helps these children become more confident, which is the antidote to shyness. A parent of one of my students introduced me to *The Whole Brain Child*, by Daniel J. Siegel, M.D. In the book, Siegel scientifically backs up exactly what I see. "Researchers who study human personality tell us that shyness is to a large extent genetic. It's actually a part of a person's core makeup present at birth. However, that doesn't mean that shyness isn't changeable to a significant degree. In fact, the way parents handle their child's shyness has a big impact on how the child deals with that aspect of his or her personality, as well as how shy the child is later on."[3] You can assist your child by teaching these lessons, rather than repeatedly telling people, "Oh, he's just shy," which is more often than not a self-fulfilling prophecy. And I'm not the only one who believes debilitating shyness can be prevented: the parent who suggested Siegel's book to me had himself been shy as a child, and he wanted to make an intervention so that his son's shyness would not be inhibiting to him.

Based on what children have written in their journals regarding first impressions A and B, go over the key aspects of making a good non-verbal first impression and review the following:

EYE CONTACT. Be sure that your kids are making eye contact for the entire introduction. Explain that it's not always easy to make eye contact, but that it is an important indicator of both confidence and respect, and that it also conveys engagement in the interaction. Ask your child to hold eye contact with you or a sibling for 15 seconds and count as you look at each other (also let them know that they can blink, so that it doesn't turn into a stare down!) This exercise bolsters confidence in making eye contact for future introductions. Use the timer on your phone or a stopwatch to make the activity even more fun.

SMILE. A smile says you're happy to meet someone, and everyone loves to feel like people are happy to meet them.

Ask kids to show you a genuine smile, and then a disingenuous smile, and then introduce yourself to your children without smiling to highlight the point.

GOOD BODY LANGUAGE. Square your shoulders and face the person you're meeting—this posture conveys that you are interested in the other person. Hands should be at your sides or can be crossed in front of you. Oftentimes kids don't know what to do with their hands and wind up swinging their hands, playing with pockets, or twirling their hair.

Give an example of good body language versus negative body language and ask the kids to show you their own examples. If you are working with more than one child, have them take turns to show everyone.

HOW TO SHAKE HANDS

In the United States, another key part of the non-verbal first impression is the handshake. It says so much about you without speaking at all. But first and foremost, do you know where the American custom of shaking hands comes from? As the saying goes, "Knowledge is power." So before we get started on how to properly shake hands, let's get a grasp on the history of greetings and why our culture shakes hands instead of kissing cheeks or bowing as other cultures do—kids will love these fun facts too!

GREETINGS IN OTHER CULTURES

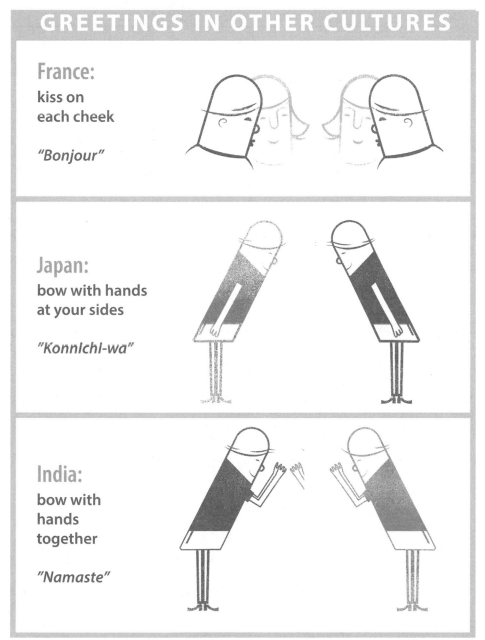

France:
**kiss on
each cheek**

"Bonjour"

Japan:
**bow with hands
at your sides**

"Konnichi-wa"

India:
**bow with
hands
together**

"Namaste"

History of the Handshake:
Conveying Trust, Balance, and Equality

The handshake predates written history, so it's hard to come up with a definitive explanation, but many stories (both spiritual and comedic) exist to explain its origin. The most plausible explanation comes from medieval times, when an open right hand indicated that one was not carrying a weapon. If two men met and displayed empty right hands, each could assume that the other would not attack him.

A similar rendition of the handshake existed in ancient Greece, where men engaged in an elbow to wrist pat down to check for hidden daggers, eventually ending with the two men clutching hands. Another explanation is that actually shaking the hand was a way to dislodge any sharp objects that may have been hidden in the adversary's sleeve. (Since women did not traditionally carry weapons, handshaking wasn't a common tradition for them.) These variations of the handshake have evolved into the handshake as we know it today.

Nuts and Bolts of the Shake

I'm sure you've met people who even as adults have awkward, weak, or just downright bad handshakes, so let's start by ensuring that neither you nor your child will be one of them! Think about that gentleman who gave you the "fingertips-only" handshake or the woman whose hand was as limp as a wet noodle. Share with your children those experiences and what impression you got when you shook hands.

When teaching your child how to properly shake hands, first empower him or her with the knowledge of the imperative components of a handshake. Explain that these are the non-verbal parts of a first impression, which are equally as important as the verbal components. As you go through each, demonstrate that action.

RIGHT HAND. In America, we always shake with our right hand.

Show kids what happens when you offer your left hand to their right hand.

STAND UP! Standing up to shake hands with someone shows respect for yourself and others.

Ask children to shake your hand while you're seated and then show them the difference when you stand up.

WEB-TO-WEB (see diagram at right).

Connect the web between your index finger and thumb firmly with the other person's.

Offering just your fingertips is what I call a "Queen's handshake," which conveys superi-

ority; putting your hand on top of someone else's hand indicates aggression.

Show kids what web-to-web is and then show what happens when you don't use your web. Ask them how it feels and which feels better. Nearly every child says it feels better when the webs touch.

SHAKE THREE TO FOUR TIMES. The shake should be neither too long, nor too short—three to four shakes usually does the trick. The idea is to shake up and down rather than forward and backward in a sawing motion.

Demonstrate how ridiculous it becomes when someone just keeps on shaking without letting go. Explain that it's important to keep one's elbow close to one's body, rather than out like a wing.

NOT TOO CLOSE (AND NOT TOO FAR). Stand approximately one straight arm's length away from the person you're meeting.

Demonstrate with your child how awkward it feels to stand too close or too far away from the person you're shaking hands with. I like to exaggerate a bit here to really make the point.

MAKE EYE CONTACT. Making eye contact while shaking hands not only helps you to remember the other person's face, but it also will help them to remember yours, and it allows you to better connect with the other person.

Demonstrate what happens when everything else is perfect, but there's no eye contact. At this juncture, I always bring up with kids that there are a number of key aspects of the first impression and if just one is missing, such as eye contact, you miss the boat on making that great first impression.

SMILE :-) "Hello, my name is FIRST NAME LAST NAME"

It's important to say your last name as well, so be sure to point that out. If, like me, you have a challenging last name, it's even more important to make sure there is a pause between the first and last name so that the person you're meeting can distinguish between the two. After the other person introduces himself or herself, we say, "It's nice to meet you!" For more advanced or older children, ask that they repeat the person's name. For example, "It's nice to meet you, John." Not only do people love to hear their own names, but stating the name again shows that you care and will also help you remember names.

Greetings can be tailored to the environment. No doubt your children have seen our President and First Lady use the "fist bump," which might be appropriate for children to use with each other. Talk through scenarios where a formal shake would be best, and others where an informal high-five or "bump" would be a fine choice.

Shakes You Never Want to Have

THE PUMPER: The shake that keeps on going, and going. . . and going!

THE TERMINATOR: Knuckle-crunching shake that may elicit a wince or a comment from the recipient

THE AGGRESSOR: Puts hand on top of your hand

THE QUEEN: A half shake or a "dainty" shake

THE DEAD FISH: Limp, bland shake. A weak handshake conveys a lack of self-confidence. Demonstrate a dead fish versus a firm shark!

THE ATHLETE: This is when hands are clasped in the air at chest level, a variation on the high-five. It is appropriate after a game, but not for everyday use.

For older kids, remind them that initiating a handshake shows confidence and respect for others.

WHAT TO SAY

Review some examples of common icebreakers with your child:

Adults or Kids:

How are you? How is your day going? Are you enjoying this beautiful weather? How was your weekend? What are you doing this weekend?

Kid Questions:

What grade are you in? What school do you go to? Do you play any sports? Do you play any instruments?

In Chapter 2 we'll discuss how to start and maintain conversations, but for now, just cover the basics of what to say when first meeting an adult or a child.

As you go over this lesson and any other in this book, keep in mind that this is your opportunity to set the tone for your household for how you'd like your children to greet others when they're out in public. Also, there may be something specific you've noticed that your child needs to work on. This is the time do address it, rather than correcting it while it's happening. I've had a few students with particular idiosyncrasies that needed to be addressed, such as one older student who tended to tilt his head back as he introduced himself, which conveyed an air of superiority.

Greeting Adults and Authority Figures

We meet and greet differently when encountering adults, teachers, parents, doctors, or presidents, and we use titles to show respect. What is respect? Kids generally know what respect is, but have a hard time verbalizing it. Dictionary.com says that respect is "deference to a right, privilege, superior position, of someone or something considered to have certain rights or privileges; proper acceptance or courtesy; acknowledgment: respect for a suspect's right to counsel; to show respect for the flag; respect for the elderly." Talk about what this means.

Titles can vary from Mr. and Mrs., to Doctor, Professor, Officer, Captain, Sister,

Father, Rabbi, President, and numerous others. Some of them are obvious while others are not quite as evident. The bottom line is that titles are used to show respect.

Have children open journals to write down the varying adult titles.

What to Call Her?

Titles for women are far from clear-cut. We use Mrs. for married women, and Miss (*sss* sound) for a girl who is younger than 18 years old. In some situations young children will refer to female school teachers as "Miss" plus the first name—Miss Faye, for example—and in the American South this is even more common with women in general. But Ms. (with a *zzz* sound) can apply to any woman, regardless of marital status. The "Ms." designation has become increasingly common in the workplace as the equivalent to the male title "Mr.," as neither is marital status–specific. Ask children how we know if someone is married. Most kids respond by saying that you can tell by checking to see if the person wears a wedding ring. You need to explain that we can't assume we know marital status simply because someone wears or does not wear a ring. When in doubt, it's best to remove the guesswork and use the prefix "Ms." for any woman. Properly greeting adults is challenging, and I think it's best to keep it as simple and uniform as possible. Review the "zzz" sound once again. It is Ms. Jones or Ms. Smith, not Ms. Jennifer Smith or Ms. Jennifer. Explain that no adult should be called by his or her first name unless they say that it's okay to do so.

Ask kids about people in their lives who go by a title other than Mr. or Ms., and ask kids to name them.

Stress with your children that they should avoid inauthenticity: people can sense in a second if their greeting is overly enthusiastic. Feel free to show your kids an example. There's the overdone, "Oh my GOSH, it's SOOOOOOOO great to see you! I love your shirt!" At the other end of the spectrum is the deflating, completely bland greeting without expression or vocal inflection. Show how impolite it can sound to speak in a monotone or maintain a neutral facial expression.

◖◖ REVIEW AND PRACTICE ◗◗

Now it's time to try out this new skill. Ask children to each take a turn doing two first impressions, just as you did at the beginning of the lesson. Kids really enjoy giving a "bad" first impression and will take great delight in it. After the second impression, ask how each of those first impressions felt. Explain that it takes practice to perfect a first impression and that it's something that will come with time. If you have anything anecdotal you can add, it can make the lesson even more poignant. I always share the story of the "Belly Button Observer" with younger kids. I once met someone who looked only at my belly button, and I show kids how awkward it feels to meet someone who doesn't look at your eyes when meeting you and just looks at your belly button. With older children, I ask if they've ever met someone who didn't make eye contact while talking, and then I point out that it conveys to the other person that something or someone else is more important than the person standing right in front of them. Point out the things that your child did well and have your child write out things that he or she is going to improve upon.

Review the journal entry in which your children wrote the key positive (and negative) aspects of a good first impression and then request that they introduce themselves to you and start a conversation. Ensure that your kids address you as "Ms." or "Mr." plus your surname. Often when they hear me introduce myself, they'll repeat back to me, "Hello, Ms. Faye de Muyshondt," but ask them to say "Ms. de Muyshondt," without the first name.

As part of this lesson, be sure to also discuss occasions other than meeting and greeting during which we shake hands: when we part ways, offer congratulations, express gratitude, or make an agreement. In sports or other competitive activities, it's also done as a sign of good sportsmanship—and is often appropriately modified as a high-five rather than as a formal shake. Demonstrate how that looks: "Congratulations on your graduation!"

Fun fact: Unless health issues or local customs dictate otherwise, a handshake should always be made using bare hands. In some regions, especially in continental Europe, attempting to perform a handshake while wearing gloves may be seen as inappropriate or even as derogatory behavior. So if it's freezing cold in your neck of the woods, as it is here in New York City during the winters, the right hand glove should be removed to shake hands.

APPLICATION AND GOALS

I suggest that this week, each time your children enter and leave the household, they need to shake hands with you. You can modify the introduction with, "Hi, Ms. LAST NAME, it's great to see you." And the departure can be, "It was great to see you, Ms. LAST NAME. Thanks for having me." Practice, as I mentioned, is so important here. Look at your week ahead and challenge your children to make as many good first impressions as they can—perhaps a few with peers and then at least one with an adult. And once they've done so, ask them to write about it in their journal: With whom did they shake hands? How did it go? What worked well? What needed improvement? How did it feel?

2

Face to Facebook: The Digital First Impression

"Legal scholars, technologists and cyber thinkers are wrestling with the first great existential crisis of the digital age: the impossibility of erasing your posted past, starting over, moving on."[1]

—Jeffrey Rosen, "The Web Means the End of Forgetting"

I've always loved kids and teaching. My first entrepreneurial venture was Faye's Babysitting, and I distributed flyers in mailboxes throughout my neighborhood. It became a bona fide business that I operated, sometimes with three jobs a day. I did the scheduling out of my bedroom, where I installed my very own phone line and answering machine (largely because my mom was fielding so many calls). Later, at Boston College, I began teaching English as a Second Language as a volunteer at a community center in the city. I loved it, but I didn't quite understand how much teaching fulfilled me until later in life.

After college, I fulfilled my childhood dream of moving to New York City to be a "career woman." I had majored in communications, and after a spectacular evening class with Professor McKinney, who ran her own PR firm, I had no doubt in my mind that PR was my career of choice. I had two positive internship experiences, one in Boston the other in New York City, and was offered a position at the international PR firm Brown Lloyd James. After working my way up to Vice-President there, I decided to set off on my own and start my own PR business. It was then that I got to the "big picture" stage in my life and realized that I missed teaching. And after discovering that a total career switch wasn't feasible, I decided to figure out how to compromise. Soon after, I began teaching an evening class at NYU based on my professional experience. I joined the NYU teaching staff as an Adjunct Professor in the department of Media,

Culture, and Communications, teaching Public Relations 101 (how to manage reputations, garner media attention, and build brands), which is where the idea for socialsklz:-) was born.

As part of my PR 101 class, students were required to build out social media campaigns for a designated brand or company. During that time, I requested that they "friend" me on Facebook for a ten-day period during which I'd monitor the progress of their social media campaign projects. Well, I ended up seeing more than their campaigns, and what I saw on my Facebook newsfeed raised many red flags. While the nature of social media is fun and, well, very social, I'd often see inappropriate photos from weekends, tawdry status updates, and "questionable" language.

I interact regularly on Facebook with various people, both personally and professionally, but I was often shocked by these students' posts. I realized that it was my responsibility to take charge. One day, I walked into class and told students we were going "off syllabus." I asked them to put away their notebooks and laptops and announced that it was time to have a dialogue—no devices allowed—to review a set of guidelines and parameters for social media. I explained that messages and posts on the Internet are often saved permanently: what you do online has the potential to live there forever. The "curtain" of a computer screen can make you believe you have total anonymity, but the reality is that an impulsive comment, photo, or blog post can result in long-term damage to one's reputation. And in a tough job market, a few reckless words could potentially be a deal breaker for securing interviews. One's online reputation is as important as one's in-person reputation—and today, it is sometimes even more important.

I shared with my students a recent Microsoft survey which revealed that seventy-five percent of human resource recruiters do Internet research on job candidates. And what's more, seventy percent of recruiters in the United States report that they have rejected potential candidates after an Internet search without even giving the candidate's résumé a glance.[2]

Since that day in class, I've read about employees who have been fired because of a post on Facebook, athletes who have been banned from the Olympic Games for impulsive tweets, and politicians who have been brought down with social media. Countless articles and even full length books have been written on the permanent record the Internet has created. In a compelling article in *The New York Times*, "The Web Means the End of Forgetting," Jeffrey Rosen eloquently pinpoints this new reality, which is so important that I also used a shortened version to open this chapter: "Legal scholars, technologists and cyber thinkers are wrestling with the first great existential crisis of the digital age: the impossibility of erasing your posted past, starting over, moving on." Rosen points out, "We live in a permissive era, one with infinite second chances. But the truth is that for a great many people, the permanent memory bank of the Web increasingly means that there are no second chances—no opportunities to escape a scarlet letter in your digital past. Now the worst thing you've done is often the first thing everyone knows about you."[3] Rosen refers to *Delete: The Virtue of Forgetting in the Digital Age*, by Viktor Mayer-Schönberger, which discusses the value of "societal forgetting," a phenomenon that is becoming nearly impossible today as a result of the Internet.

In "Erasing the Digital Past," published in *The New York Times*, Nick Bilton highlights examples of individuals who posted photos of themselves that have effectively "metastasized" like cancer, and are now virtually impossible to delete because the data has "embedded itself into the nether reaches of cyberspace, etched into the archives, algorithms, and a web of hyperlinks."[4] And while there is talk of erasing one's digital trail after ten years, it isn't yet a reality. So it is vital that we parents assertively guide our children to ensure that they don't end up wearing a scarlet letter in their digital lives.

Occasionally, when a parent calls our office to sign up their kids for our socialtweenz program, they ask if their kids can skip the Internet Safety and Savvy portion of the workshop because they haven't yet allowed their children to use the Internet. My first question is, "Why not start the education early?" Teaching our children about the advantages and perils of the Internet is vital; if you can, you should start before kids actually go online. After all, they're already surrounded by Internet applications, have heard the word "Google" used as a verb, and likely have seen you emailing, using Facebook, and texting.

We spend so much time teaching our children the basics of life. We help them journey through diapers and pull-ups to the potty, we teach them to ride a tricycle and how to balance on a bicycle, and we accompany them for years as they walk to school, until we finally become comfortable with letting them go off on their own. And yet most parents never sit down at a computer with their kids to teach them about one of the most useful and potentially dangerous tools that they will use for the rest of their lives: the Internet. We all want the best for our children, and an important part of that is setting them up for success online. This chapter will guide you toward effectively teaching your kids how to be safe, savvy, and independent in the virtual world, just as we try to do in the real world.

Five Common Mistakes Children Make Online

- **Forgetting that the Internet is a permanent database**
- **Feeling "anonymous" when commenting or sending messages online**
- **Participating in social media channels indiscriminately**
- **Sharing passwords with friends**
- **Giving out personal information like their address, full name, and age**

LESSON

By the end of this chapter, your children will have a solid understanding of the many ways in which we interact on the Web, and how important it is that they interact cautiously. They will grasp the concept that they always need to think before typing and that they must adhere to guidelines before they're set free to navigate the Wild Wild Web.

❧ INTERNET SAFETY AND SAVVY ☙

The most important part of teaching this lesson is creating an atmosphere of trust. I typically open this portion of the class by discussing what an incredibly valuable tool the Internet is. I also share how much I do online and how it has enhanced my life in many respects. When parents get involved with kids online, they often get a negative response because kids think parental involvement means restrictions. Share with your children all the great things that the Internet has done for you and what life was like pre-Internet. It gets the lesson off on the right foot. This is not just a lecture on the dangers of the Internet. Instead, it's the foundation for getting kids ready to operate independently online without the dreaded POS (parents over shoulders) or PAW (parents are watching). Kids are eager to go online on their own, so once you have confidence in their ability to do so safely, everyone wins.

For the work in this chapter, I suggest having a computer available. Hands-on learning will help you to demonstrate the practical applications of the lessons, and will be interactive and fun. For starters, it's important to know about your children's online activity. You might have the advantage of knowing what your children do at home, but you may not be aware of what they do at school or at friends' homes. Try to be as judgment-free as you can and allow this to be an open forum for getting to know what they're up to. (In case your kids aren't yet online, we've provided applicable sample questions below for them, too.)

⟪⟪ QUESTIONNAIRE ⟫⟫

Have children open their journals (if you're using your own journal, add a new entry heading for Internet Safety). Start the lesson by explaining that you're going to ask a few questions and request that your child write responses in his or her journal. If you don't feel that there is an atmosphere of trust, remind your children that this is a fun activity and that they're not going to be in trouble for anything they write. Here are a few sample questions.

FOR KIDS WHO ARE ALREADY ONLINE: What are your favorite websites to visit when you go on the Internet? Do you play games online? Who do you email the most? Have you ever had something strange or creepy pop up on the computer that you didn't mean to open? What's cyber-bullying? What's social media? Do you talk to anyone online? What do you search on Google?

FOR KIDS WHO ARE NOT YET ONLINE: What do you want to do on the Internet when you begin using it? Will you play games? What is social media? What is Facebook? What do you think "netiquette" means? What's bullying online? What is a chat room?

∞ EMAIL ∞

Most kids know about email, and practically every young adult has an email address. If your children aren't emailing yet, explain what it is, as well as when and why you email people. Share with your child that it is an effective and useful tool and that it's a great way to communicate, although picking up the phone and speaking in-person is a terrific way to communicate as well. As your children get older, their email addresses (and emails) will commonly serve as first impressions to other people, especially when they're emailing peers, teachers, and eventually potential employers.

Fun Fact:
294 billion emails
are sent each day, and some
90 trillion emails
are sent each year.

Opening an email account is a pretty big deal and should be done properly and with the knowledge in hand to manage it responsibly. Just as is the case with every other account a child opens online, creating an email account must be done with a parent or with parental approval. If your child is already actively emailing, I suggest you use this lesson as a thorough review of any accounts he or she has already set up.

Email addresses are also important because they will potentially stay with your children for a very long time. An email handle is limited only by the imagination: PrincessFairy@gmail.com or HulkHenry@yahoo.com. But be sure to ask your children if they would be comfortable using that same email address when they're teenagers or when they're adults. If the answer is no, then it's not the right one. Although kids might be inclined to have an email address that reflects a certain hobby or object of affection, it's important to ask if they think it could potentially be embarrassing later in life.

Go over what makes an email address appropriate: simplicity, authenticity, and timelessness are key. Throughout their lives, children will say their email addresses countless times in person, over the phone, on the playground, and in so many other settings. People with unique last names, like mine, will have an easier time securing an email address using their first and last names. For example, to date, there aren't any other Faye de Muyshondts out there, so acquiring fayedemuyshondt@gmail.com is very likely possible. However, people with more common names may need to be a bit more creative. The most important thing is that children use their names rather than creative nick-names, princess titles, superhero references, or acronyms.

Here are some examples of unfortunate past email addresses of our own staff members, names that ended up causing them embarrassment after their teenage years:

socckaplaya123@gmail.com

gossipgrl1983@hotmail.com

luscious_cherry_babe@yahoo.com

cute.kitti@verizon.net

fluffyfairy@aol.com.

My maiden name was Rogaski and my very first email address was fayerog@aol.com. Unfortunately, there are still a few people who call me "fayerog" or "frog."

What specifically makes these email addresses a bad choice? First, you wouldn't want to apply for a job using any of those addresses (which I quickly learned); second, when you deliberately misspell a word like "soccer" it isn't easy to verbally convey the address to someone; third, all of the above addresses are practically begging to be made fun of. Ask your children to come up with a few appropriate email addresses in their journals, and if you want to have a little fun, come up with a few inappropriate ones too. Encourage children to write down an email entry in their journals and include what their email address is or what they would like for their next email address to be.

Also, as you set up an email address with your children, be certain that the "Name" field isn't the email address itself; for example, "fayedemuyshondt@gmail.com." Instead, it should be your child's actual name: Faye de Muyshondt or de Muyshondt, Faye. (This is a good time to check your own email account: be sure that your smart phone emails are coming from the same name as your computer emails. It's terribly annoying when you can't find an email because the sender is sending under different names— "Faye de Muyshondt," as well as "de Muyshondt, Faye," and then "fayedemuyshondt@gmail.com." Make the name you're sending from universal!)

The next item to review is how to send a proper email. Although it's unpleasant to think that your emails will have an unintended recipient, it's bound to happen. You can explain to children how easy it is to forward emails, how they can be printed out, and how they can be shared with an entire school, parents, or a principal. An email should be treated as if it could be read by anyone, as if it were no different than a postcard. Set up a mock email template with your children in their journals, including the To, From, CC:, BCC:, and Subject Line. Even if your kids aren't yet emailing, you want to ensure they know how to email properly when the time comes.

SAMPLE EMAIL

To:

From:

CC:

BCC:

Subject:

BODY

FIRST THINGS FIRST. A subject line is very important. An email without a subject line could easily go unread. Explain that this is a practice email that will be from your child to his or her teacher and it will extend thanks to the teacher. In this case, the subject line would be "Thank You." A thank-you email is one that has a much higher probability of being read immediately than one with the subject line, "Your Payment to American Express is Due!"

NEXT REVIEW "CC" AND "BCC." "CC" stands for "carbon copy," and dates back to a time when typists used a sheet of carbon paper to make duplicate copies. While I don't suggest trying to explain that to your children, I'd suggest that you explain that CC is used to send a copy of the email to others. Share an example of when that might be useful—perhaps an email to a friend confirming a sleepover with the date, time, and address, in which the parents are copied on the email. Explain why it's useful to copy parents on that email. Additionally, talk about the difference between "Reply" and "Reply All" when responding to emails with numerous recipients. You might want to stress that this is a common mistake and that it can have serious consequences. Suggest to your child that it's always a good idea to take a moment to consider to whom he or she is responding. Explain that if you select "Reply All" you are sending the message to every recipient listed in the email. If the original email was sent to, say, a dozen people, you will be replying to all of them, some of whom you may not know. If you select "Reply," you are sending the message only to the one person who sent out the email. Take a moment to explain "BCC", too. It can be useful to "blind-copy" several recipients in an invitation or announcement, or to plan an event.

Although most children between the ages of 7 and 12 might not be interacting with their friends over email on a regular basis, it is important that they follow certain guidelines when they do. Review with your child that a first-time email to anyone, especially an adult, should be done formally—similar to the way a letter would be written, with an opening and closing. Emails with friends can and should be casual and fun, but many of my students at NYU email me in the same way they would email a classmate to grab food after class—no punctuation, sentence fragments, and "totes" full of "abbrevs." Ask kids to write out their formal email in their journal using the formal letter format that they may have learned in school. The computer can become a distraction during the lesson, so it's easier to focus on the email if kids write it out in their journals. We'll write an actual email at the end of the chapter.

HERE IS A SAMPLE OF THE FORMAT FOR A FORMAL EMAIL:

From: faye@socialsklz.com

To: Nadine.E.Brown@hotmail.com

CC: Jenny Brown@hotmail.com

BCC:

Subject: Thank You

Dear Ms. Brown,

I wanted to say thank you so much for taking me to lunch with you and Jenny on Monday. I had a really nice time and loved spending time with both of you. I enjoyed learning more about your job and what you do at the bakery shop. I look forward to seeing you soon.

Best,

Faye de Muyshondt

❧ SOCIAL MEDIA ☙

Social media has become part of the fabric of American teens' lives, and each year there are a few new social media sites to be sure you're aware of. If you're not active on social media, you should at the very least familiarize yourself with it. So often kids' interactions with each other are playing out online, rather than in the schoolyard, and in order to guide and protect your children, you need to understand the game.

According to a study done by the Pew Research Center, "fully 95% of all teens ages 12 to 17 are now online and 80% of those online teens are users of social media sites."[5] Just like keeping abreast of your child's friends, knowing where your child is spending time online is a significant part of modern-day parenting. Arm yourself with all the knowledge that you can. And while you're at it "like" us on Facebook (www.facebook.com/socialsklz) and feel free to share any anecdotes from your experiences using the book. We post on a daily basis (and we also tweet @socialsklz) so you'll get to see what I'm up to as well.

Although the term "social media" might perplex your younger children, the term "Facebook" won't. If you're on Facebook, surely you've had KOS (kids over shoulders) while perusing your newsfeed on your smart phone or computer. They've heard the term used in your household or when you're on the phone. Pretty soon, if it hasn't happened already, the tables will turn and you'll be the one watching your kids type "POS" (Parents over Shoulders) in their messages.

Various social media platforms provide a multitude of new ways for us to communicate with each other through photos, status updates, 140-character tweets, and for the more verbose, blog posts. Explain to your kids that social media is yet another revolution in the way that we communicate with each other, and point out that, as is the case in every other revolution, there are winning and losing aspects, as well as some "casualties."

In order to get the lesson off to the right start, open up your Facebook account and explain that the nature of social media is fun and—as the name suggests—social. This means that more people can communicate with each other than ever before, at all hours of the day, and all over the world. There are enormous benefits to being able to communicate with your family members and friends who live across the globe, as well as with people whom we couldn't previously keep in contact. However, as with anything in life, there are certain guidelines that we all need to follow when using social media.

For all intents and purposes, I'm going to use Facebook as the social media of choice for this lesson, as most children will have a Facebook account early on. As of this writing, children must technically be 13 years old to have a Facebook account, although Facebook is working on a younger version, and of course there are already children younger than 13 on Facebook.

Let's start with what's appropriate and inappropriate for sharing on social media sites.

Wall Posts

Mention that, by default, things you post on other people's walls can be seen not only by your Facebook friends, but by all the other person's friends. Show an example of a friend who wrote on someone else's wall. The same thing goes for photos: if you're tagged in a photo, it will show up in other people's news-feeds and in your own photo album section of Facebook.

Privacy Settings

Emphasize to your children how important these settings are. They allow you to choose who sees all the information you're posting on Facebook; you can choose what Facebook friends and non-Facebook friends can see, and can even choose what information gets shown to different groups of your Facebook friends. For example, you can decide to set all your wall posts and photos to be visible only to your friends—or you can even make them visible only to certain friends: book club friends, tennis friends, or another group. But just because you can set up privacy restrictions doesn't mean you shouldn't carefully consider whether each post or photo is appropriate for using online. If a child wants his or her friends to see a post but doesn't want Grandma to see it, be very clear: it's not appropriate to post. If your children haven't yet set up accounts on Facebook, you have the opportunity to properly set up their privacy settings. If children are already on Facebook, I'd suggest checking to see what is and is not private from other users. Facebook is constantly changing privacy settings, and it's imperative to regularly check in to see that your child's profile remains private.

Photos

Smartphones and digital cameras make it easy to take photos anywhere, anytime, and any place. And while some are perfect for sharing, others can easily be embarrassing. Discuss with your children what types of photos are suitable for sharing.

Before posting photos on the Internet, it's a great practice to ask permission from the people in them. At the same time, review in the privacy settings of Facebook the "photo review" tag that allows you to be alerted before someone tags you in any photo. At the very least, this feature allows you to refuse the tag in an unflattering photo. However, it's important to point out that people can still view your online photos, even without a tag.

The most important takeaway from this lesson on social media is that we shouldn't say or post anything that we might regret. Recently I was conducting a workshop on social media. When I went on Facebook to search students by name, I was appalled by how few of those students had adjusted their privacy settings. One of the students turned cherry-red and said "DO NOT LOOK AT MY PHOTOS!" Much to her dismay, I was free to view a number of her completely inappropriate photos and status updates. Another student had no idea that a Google search of her name produced a number of photos that she'd shared on a photo-sharing site, but had failed to set as private. During an assembly that I conducted at the Friends Seminary here in New York City, a student told me that he uses another name on Facebook. Do not let your children do this. Owning what they write and share online is vital. Besides, an alias can easily be traced back to your children.

Blogs, Comments, and Chatting Online

Since most children in the 7-12 age bracket are in the pre-blogging stage, it's likely that they're not writing their own blogs. But they may be commenting on other people's blogs or websites and chatting with their friends. Kids can access millions of different blog posts and view sites about pretty much everything, ranging from unicorns to video games to "the cinnamon challenge" (beware!). The most important thing you can teach your children is that no matter how "anonymous" their user name may seem, everything they post on the Internet is permanent; even if we choose to delete a comment we regret posting, it's possible that someone has already seen it, copied and posted it elsewhere on the Internet, and someone else could have seen that comment . . . the cycle never ends.

Cyber-Bullying

Last but not least, I must mention the importance of working with your children to prevent any type of inappropriate online behavior or, heaven forbid, cyber-bullying. While it seems that children have become nearly immune to the term "bullying" in the classroom, I always address the topic of thoughtfulness, respect, and empathy in the context of what we do online.

A few quick keyboard strokes or an email written in the heat of the moment too often results in kids causing harm to themselves; in extreme cases, the consequences are devastating—we've all seen the news stories. Children can feel too comfortable and quite anonymous sitting behind a computer screen in pajamas. It is essential that they give serious thought to the kinds of damage that they might incur when they write whatever comes to mind. Not only are your children responsible for their actions online, you can be held accountable too. Under a legal concept called "vicarious liability," parents can be sued in civil court for damages caused by their child's inappropriate online activity; in the worst cases, they may also face criminal charges.

꧁ REVIEW AND PRACTICE ꧂

As a review of this lesson, see my "Internet Contract" on the next page, which details the ways in which a child should use the Internet responsibly. It is a contract that I go over with students and then ask them to review and sign with their parents at home. You'll likely have a few of your own points that you want to include, but I provide the basic rules here.

Discuss what you view as a reasonable amount of time for your child to be online each week. According to a recent study from the Kaiser Family Foundation, aside from time spent sleeping or in school, the average young American (8-18 years old) now spends almost every minute using a smart phone, computer, television or other electronic device. The same Kaiser study showed that heavy media use is associated with behavior problems and lower grades.[6] Human contact and in-person conversation is imperative to counter the effects of so much time online, and it's important to parlay that to kids. As actor and comedian Steve Carell says, "As human beings, we should naturally crave contact with one another. But sadly, as the world grows more and more technologically advanced, we lose our ability to connect as human beings." [7] We parents must ensure that we send our children into the world equipped to connect with others.

Because this is a lesson on managing your digital first impression, you may want to set up Google Alerts for both your name and your child's name, if you haven't already. You want to be sure that you know when anything is posted on the Internet with your name. Clearly, for those individuals with more common names it will be more difficult to find the most relevant information, but for those of us with less common names, it's easy to spot any new content. If your name is more common, set up qualifiers such as First and Last Name plus the city you live in.

⤶ APPLICATION AND GOALS ⤷

This week, set up an email account with your children, if you haven't already done so. Walking through the setup process is important for them to see as well. Review what their email addresses will be and explain how to create strong passwords, ones that are less likely to be hacked. For example, a weak password would be your child's birthday, but a strong password might be one that combines numbers and letters, both upper and lower case. Now that your children have entered a practice email in their journals, set up a list of emails

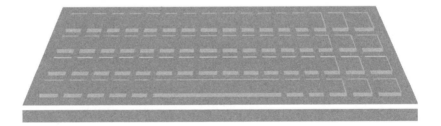

(-: **THE INTERNET CONTRACT** :-)

As I work online, I,_____, promise:

I WILL ALWAYS

...SHARE my Internet activity and ask before opening new accounts.

...ASK before downloading anything, even if a pop-up prompts me to do so.

...SHARE passwords with my parents.

...STOP before sending or posting and ask myself, "Is this appropriate?" and
"How would I feel about a similar photo of me?"

...CLOSE any web site with creepy or inappropriate photos and tell my parents.

I WILL NEVER

...SHARE personal information online, like my full name, address,
age, school name, or what I look like.

...SEND or post anything that could be hurtful or inappropriate.

...MEET in-person with someone I have met online.

to send this week: connect with a family member, or send a thank-you email to a friend. Just as you might read books to your children, spend some time together online, researching and going to sites that they might enjoy as a fun activity. This is a good opportunity to practice together and to get a good feel for what your children might, or might not, be up to in the digital world.

3

Putting a Final End to the One-Word "Conversation"

"We can have brilliant ideas,
but if you can't get them across,
your ideas won't get you anywhere."

—Lee Iacocca

A study at the Stanford University School of Business tracked a group of MBAs 10 years after they graduated. The result? Grade point averages were not a good predictor of success—but the graduates' ability to converse with others was.[1]

Don't get me wrong. I'm an advocate of giving children the best possible education, but equipping kids with good communication skills is equally, if not more, important. Just as food, clothing, and shelter are necessary for survival, I believe communication skills should be as well. Sure, it's going to be a few years before your children decide whether they'd like to pursue an MBA, but now is the time to start fostering the art of conversation. Given that relationships, both personal and professional, and social interaction are the foundation for everything else in our lives, the journey towards mastering this skill set is a worthwhile endeavor.

It has happened to all of us. One day we bump into someone we know—and an uncomfortable silence ensues, even downright awkwardness. You ask a few questions and keep getting the same one-word "yes" and "no" responses. All you want to do is run. Or perhaps you're the conversation killer: you don't know what to say, you don't know what to do, and the awkwardness feels thick enough to cut with a knife. The very same thing happens to children, but with more frequency. It's just as awkward for them, except that sometimes adults will add to the mounting discomfort, telling them to "say hello" or "make eye contact," making matters that much worse.

For many kids, conversing, let alone initiating a conversation, is downright daunting, potentially awkward, and for a few, next to impossible. And yet I see time and time again that conversation skills can be taught, practiced, and through repetition, can become second nature. These skills don't develop overnight, but once you have a basic knowledge of them, conversation will no longer be a source of angst. We don't tend to teach these skills to children; instead, we assume they will pick them up along the way, just as they do with so many of the other skills we're working on. In my view, we need to anticipate conversations and address any potential stress that might arise. There's no question about it: this lesson will truly pay off and will improve your children's current and future relationships.

Courtney Fox, the 2008 Delaware Teacher of the Year, explains, "Conversation skills are important for academic and social learning at all grade levels. The school day is full of conversations—we talk with each other in large group gatherings, at work and choice times, and of course during snack, recess, and lunch. Children who are not skilled in this arena may struggle, academically and socially. That's why it's important to teach conversation skills explicitly."[2]

Fun Fact: Did you know that we can think at about four times the speed that we can speak? That leaves time for our brains to process the meaning of what we're about to say.

Five Most Common Conversation Hurdles for Children

- Can't initiate conversation
- One-word responses
- Interrupts others
- Poor eye contact and body language
- Can't actively listen

I love teaching this lesson during our workshops because communication skills truly enhance a child's life in every regard. You will see the return on your investment, and your children will too. Children respond particularly well to this lesson; seeing them become successful in this realm is a tremendously rewarding experience, and I believe it will be for you, as well.

One of my favorite stories comes from a socialteenz workshop. At the beginning of the lesson, one young man appeared to be shy, socially uncomfortable, and self-conscious. By the end of the program, though, he seemed to have transformed; he had managed to put his skills to use between the first and second Saturdays of the workshop. It was clear that he had developed more confidence, and he promptly asked me if I could teach him how to talk to young ladies. He had deduced the value of these skills and now wanted to apply them to the very important task of chatting up girls! Knowing how to converse and make small talk builds confidence, empowers, and boosts self-esteem for every relationship in life.

Years ago, when I was in my twenties, I would see Dale Carnegie's *How to Make Friends and Influence People* in bookstores and wonder why anyone would purchase it. Why would someone need to be taught how to make friends? Years later, we're now living in the digital age and, much to my amazement, the title remains on the shelves. The book has sold approximately 30 million copies, and over 8 million people have taken Dale Carnegie workshops. I finally decided it might be worthwhile to take a look. Imagine—a book published in 1936 that is still wildly successful today! Carnegie covers such things as how to develop strong conversational skills. I don't know if I was more shocked by the fact that adults still wanted to learn these lessons, or by the fact that people hadn't already learned the lessons. In a *CBS Sunday Morning* interview, Peter V. Handal, Chairman and CEO of Dale Carnegie Training, was asked why people paid good money to learn such elementary lessons. He explained that these skills are often common sense, but that "the difference is, they are not common practice."[3] So while people might know how they should treat others, they don't necessarily apply this knowledge to their own lives.

The value of conversation cannot be underestimated. It allows children to be heard by others—teachers, peers, and us, their parents; later in life, when they're adults, it is their partners, employers, and colleagues who will be listening. The ability to converse with others is a gift, one that can open doors and make life more enjoyable and fulfilling. And it's a gift that keeps on giving. I always convey to students that these skills allow us to hear more "yeses" than "nos" when we ask for things we want. And let's face it: the ability to make small talk can make life a heck of a lot easier. In kid-friendly terms, it makes it easier to make friends and keep friends.

LESSON

By the end of this chapter, children will understand the importance of conversation. They will develop a set of conversation starters and will understand how to make conversation more comfortable.

conversationsklz:-)

As you read further in this book, take the opportunity to connect material from an earlier lesson to a current one. It builds continuity, but more importantly, making connections from one chapter to the next will help your kids retain and master a toolkit for life. For example, conversation skills are enhanced when you use good body language (page 34), and it's easier to have a conversation when two people are making eye contact (page 33).

Let's start with five incredibly important aspects of your children's conversational abilities: initiating, asking and responding to questions, showing enthusiasm, active listening, and closing a conversation. It's important to explain to children that conversation isn't acting and that there is no script. It's essential to point out that you're not asking them to be someone other than who they are. In this lesson, children practice conversation skills while being themselves, a key component to mastering the art. Ask children to start a "conversationsklz:-)" entry in their journals.

In our workshops, we like to keep things fun, so we kick off this lesson with an exercise that will strike a chord in children. I ask my students to write in their journals the following question—"How was your weekend?"—and then have them pose it to me two different times. The first time around, I answer in a monotone, with no facial expression, and with no body language cues. I simply say, "It was fine, thanks," and then there's that awkward silence. I sit very still and look at the students as the tension mounts and they begin to squirm in their seats. The second time around, I answer the same question with enthusiasm and excitement. "My weekend was pretty good. My husband, daughter, and I took a trip to visit our dear friends in the Amish country in Pennsylvania where there is a winery and then spent some time with my family and parents in New Jersey. How about you?"

In your lesson, practice the two different scenarios with your children, asking them write a response to each one in their journals. Take mental note of how your children respond to the silence in your exercise, and ask them to write about your response to the question in their journals. After they've finished writing, ask students which response was more interesting or which one they thought was "better:" unanimously, they prefer the second. Then I ask what it was in particular that they liked better, getting into the specifics of each response.

This exercise allows you to explore various ways to make conversation. First and foremost, a conversation is meant to be two people speaking, both responding and asking questions, with enthusiasm and interest. Here you can take a few moments to also point out the importance of some of the lessons in Chapter 1 that carry over into conversations, including body language and eye contact and how useful they are in making someone else feel comfortable during a conversation.

A conversation is not one person asking all the questions and only getting one-word responses from the other. On the other hand, it isn't one person doing all the talking and not asking any questions of the other person either. I always equate a conversation to a soccer game. There wouldn't be a game if one person dribbled the ball on his or her own. Passing the ball is what makes a game happen. Now model the conversation responder who doesn't stop talking and never asks a question of the initiator: highlight your point and garner a few laughs by keeping your chatterbox impression going as long as you can. Ask your children if they have ever experienced the chatterbox. In my workshops, it's not unusual to have a student who goes on so long that I end up whipping out my stopwatch as a corrective measure! You might be enlightened with a story or two from your children's very own experiences. They pick up on the comparison fairly quickly. Bottom line: a conversation is a healthy balance between two (or more) people.

Initiating and Responding to Questions

When they attempt this exercise, kids might say that they're shy, but the beauty of good conversation skills is that you can find a comfortable balance of talking and listening so that the "shy" person doesn't need to do all the talking. Additionally, in a comfortable conversation, the child who claims to be "shy" might open up, especially if he or she is talking about something he or she enjoys. If you notice that your child is nervous about starting or carrying on a conversation, share a story about a time when you felt nervous in a conversational experience. Being empathetic is a useful teaching tool and helps to create an atmosphere of understanding. Many kids feel anxious and uncertain when making conversation in public, but these feelings can be overcome with the help of this lesson and practice. It helps to view conversation skills the way you would any hobby or sport. Having the perfect golf swing or mastering the perfect forehand in tennis doesn't happen quickly; it takes hours of practice to hone the skill. The only difference is that a golf swing or a forehand will likely only be important for a certain period of life, while conversation skills will be incredibly important for the rest of your children's lives.

Explain that there are conversation starters we can use with just about anyone: for example, you can inquire about someone's meal, or about their plans for a time in the future. Some questions might be, "What did you have for lunch?" or "What are you doing after school?" Ask your children to think of a few more. Ask them to write down conversation-starter questions in their journals. If you get the "I don't know" response, don't get frustrated: it happens to the best of us. Just offer a bit of guidance with a few examples of your own: **What are you up to this weekend? What school do you go to? What did you do last weekend? How was your holiday/summer/winter break? What do you like to do in your free time?**

Another strategy is to pose a question that is related to your current setting. Let's say you see a friend at the pool. Some sample questions might be, "Are you going swimming?" or, "Is this your first time at the pool?" Once your children are done writing, review their sample questions. The idea is to demonstrate that there are questions to ask in any situation, and that making inquiries of others can not only facilitate the process of meeting people, but make it that much more fun.

We must remember, too, that at times we may encounter complex situations in which asking questions can make a conversation unpleasant or uncomfortable. These questions are usually about private topics or details that may be regarded by others as too personal. Think of some questions that are off-limits, that we don't ask anyone, and that your children should avoid—this exercise will also surely elicit a few laughs. Be sure to point out that it's entirely inappropriate to ask the following:

How much money do your parents make? How many friends do you have? Why is your house so small? Why don't your parents live together? Why do you practice that religion?

Also discuss the fact that we shouldn't ask about physical or emotional differences we notice in others: the same way we wouldn't stare or point at someone who appears different, we wouldn't draw attention to visible differences or disabilities in conversation. If children want to know why they can't ask these questions, clarify that certain matters may simply be private and that asking questions about them can make the other person feel uncomfortable or picked on.

Now that we have our questions at hand, let's move on to the important part of how to respond to questions effectively. Explain to children that they should give full responses which are enthusiastic and engaging, but without belaboring points. Here is an example:

"How was your weekend, Malia?"

"Good."

Versus:

"How was your weekend, Malia?"

"It was great, thanks. I went to the movies with my friend and had a sleepover at her house on Saturday night. On Sunday I hung out with my family. How was yours?"

The more information you provide in the response, the more interesting the conversation becomes. The goal of a conversation is to get to know someone better and it's likely that your children will be delighted to find they have things in common with the people they talk to. Remind children to offer up questions during a conversation to keep it going, instead of just talking about themselves.

Because it's important for children to show respect for adults, explain to your kids that they might want to approach their interactions with adults a bit differently. Instead of asking parents how their weekends were, a child might want to thank them for hosting a play date or for making dinner. Just as there are some types of questions children should not pose to other children, there are some questions kids should never ask an adult. Here are some examples: **How old are you? How much money do you make? Are you pregnant? Are you a Democrat or a Republican? What are your religious views? Are you married or divorced? How many carats is your diamond ring?**

With slightly older children, this lesson can be a bit more advanced. Tweens can learn how to ask questions that are more tailored to the people with whom they're conversing. For example, if they know that someone just went on vacation, likes music, is an athlete, or saw a movie, they can ask a question pertaining to one of those things. Suggest to your tween that he or she include the other person's name in the question: "How was your ski trip, Sarah?" Let your child know that using someone's name really personalizes interaction and makes other people feel good.

The responses you give are just as important as the questions you ask. One-word responses do the opposite of furthering conversation—they bring it to a halt. Have your child ask you questions so that you can show him or her some appropriate ways to respond. As an example, I often provide two separate responses to the question, "Where do you live?" Here's an example of a limited response: "I live on East 58th Street." And here is a more appropriate response: "I live at Columbus Circle, really close to the park. It's great because I go to the park every day with my dog, Mica Girl. What about you?" It's important to note that a response doesn't go on and on. . . and on. We have a window of time to respond and then the conversation needs to be passed off to your partner, just as you would pass a baton in a relay race.

Listening

Katie Couric's *The Best Advice I Ever Got* includes some advice from television and radio host Larry King. "I never learned anything when I was talking. The best learning lesson I can give you on accomplishment is to listen. Learn how to listen. You don't learn anything when you are talking. Think about it."[4]

Listening is essential to mastering the art of conversation. You're listening to get to know the other person and, as Larry King put it, it's hard to learn anything while you're talking. I've often heard people say, "God gave us two ears and one mouth so we should listen twice as much as we talk." We've all been in the uncomfortable position in which we're talking but it seems that the other person isn't listening. And at times we've probably also felt pretty confident that the other person was listening and responding. It's easy to recognize the clues that someone is actively listening: eye contact, open body language, an engaged facial expression, nodding one's head or interjecting a few words of encouragement— "Yeah, I know," or just, "Uh huh?" And there are tell-tale signs that someone is not listening, including crossed arms, avoiding eye contact, a blank stare, fidgeting, or pausing before responding. Take a moment and have children write in their journals some of the ways they can be active listeners. Talk with them about how good it feels when you can tell that someone is listening and how good we make other people feel when we're genuinely listening.

While the other person is speaking, it's important to really be listening rather than focusing on what you're going to say or allowing other thoughts to distract you, which leads to interrupting others. This is a skill set that is invaluable because it is one of the easiest ways to show someone that you really care about them; that said, it is one that involves a degree of self-control which can be a challenge for children. All skills take time to develop, so don't be frustrated if there aren't instantaneous results for your child. The art of conversation is complex, but with practice and repetition in everyday life, you will see results.

With older children, you can get into the more advanced active listening technique in which you reflect or paraphrase what the speaker just said. That doesn't mean you can just parrot the speaker's words back to him or her: it takes creativity to come up with appropriate paraphrases in response to what we've heard. Start by asking your children to tell you about an event or an achievement—say, their experience winning a soccer game—and then paraphrase back to them to show how you understood the key point of their story: "Wow, it must have been incredible to have made that important pass." Ask your children to do the same with a story that you tell.

How to Close a Conversation

Ending a conversation can seem like bad manners. In practice, if you do it well, it will be satisfying for both participants. We've all been in a position in which a conversation seems interminable, but neither party knows how to close it.

Start a conversation with your child, keeping it going for a minute or so, and then pause uncomfortably, and say, "So, uh. . . " Look around the room, and act as if you have no idea what to say next. Once you've made your point— how uncomfortable it can be when neither party will step up and politely say goodbye—practice again, closing the conversation as follows, "Well, it was great talking to you and I hope you have a nice afternoon." Model that same conversation closing, but add a handshake. Ask children which they thought was preferable, and why.

Explain that you should avoid interrupting the speaker when closing a conversation. Let the other person finish what they're saying before you begin. You don't need a reason to close, and it's not worth making up an excuse for leaving. ("Oh, I hear someone calling me!") That only gets us in trouble down the road. Ask kids to write a journal entry for conversation closers, specifying that they should make up a few other phrases they can use. You can use the basic, "It was great talking with you," but you can also wrap up the topic at hand. For example, "Well, Tom, I hope that your birthday party is terrific. Enjoy the rest of your day."

REVIEW AND PRACTICE

Ask children to review what they learned in Chapter 1 on introductions (page 30) before you get started. Explain that for the practice activity, they will have to introduce themselves and then start a conversation with you. If you have a few children, they can practice with each other as well. Give your children a few minutes to review conversation starters in their journals so that they're prepared.

It's pretty much a given that children will need to do the exercise a few times to get everything right. The first time around, you can be the initiator. Introduce yourself and then ask your first question to begin a conversation. Try using a "talking stick" to make it easy to determine whose turn it is. Each person can hold a potato, a tennis ball, or a hacky sack, and then pass it to the next person whose turn it is. Every 20 seconds, pass the object so that no one ends up hogging the conversation. Try to ask meaningful questions, and attempt to maintain the conversation for a minute or two, passing the object back and forth. Just be sure that it doesn't turn into a game of "hot potato."

Keep your approach light-hearted, and have fun with the activity too. There is a lot for your child to master here, both from this lesson and from Chapter 1. For example, if your child forgets to stand up before introducing him or herself, stop and ask, "Wait, what's missing here?" During workshops, my most effective tactics include dramatizing people's mistakes to highlight how awkward it can be socially. As you review the exercise, I try to be funny when I highlight what's missing. The more dramatic your demeanor, the more dramatic the learning experience.

This next exercise is a review of listening skills. Put away the "talking stick" so there are no distractions and make it clear that you'll both be working on listening skills. Ask your child to review the behavior that indicates engaged listening. Then repeat your proper introductions and start a new conversation. This time, instead of focusing on taking turns and asking questions, the spotlight is on active listening and retaining information. Tell a story, something new and different with a few fun details that children might retain. Then pause and ask your child a question pertaining to your story. And then work on how your child might ask a question pertaining to the details of the story that would show he or she was actively listening.

For the more advanced tweens, you can also try a paraphrasing exercise. To start, let your child initiate by asking a question to which you will respond with a short story or anecdote. Then ask him or her to paraphrase it back to you, offering guidance, if necessary. Now reverse the exercise and paraphrase back to your child.

I recall taking the Barclay classes as a child, which taught dancing and social interactions in a formal setting. Although they were focused on teaching essential dance steps, our instructor would also weave in a few opportunities to observe details about our surroundings, to teach us to pay attention. I remember one time when I was dancing with my partner, Richard, and our instructor intervened. He turned to Richard and asked if he could describe my necklace (I was wearing a single strand of pearls). Although Richard couldn't answer the question, it was a lifelong lesson on paying attention to details, just as we do while others are speaking.

For the final review, go over with your child how to close a conversation politely and effectively, without any awkwardness.

⟪ APPLICATION AND GOALS ⟫

Children will become more and more comfortable with practice. This lesson provides a foundation that will allow them to converse in any setting. The ultimate goal is to be spontaneous and natural in conversation, a skill that will develop as your children start to feel more at ease when talking with others.

For now, set some practical goals for the week ahead. Consider instituting a new household rule: before any event or outing, ask your children to prepare three things to ask the friends and family that you will see throughout the upcoming week. Review those questions each time you leave the house, and you can even check the questions off the list after your child asks them. Set these goals based on what your schedule looks like and write them down in the journal. If you're attending a birthday party, for example, that's a great opportunity for your children to start a conversation with someone about the party itself: where they came up with the theme, how they like the presents, or even the flavor of the cake.

With the older age set, have some fun by studying people on television. Take out your journal and spend an evening on the couch watching a newscast. Specifically, focus on the anchor and the person being interviewed. Ask a few questions: How did that person make you feel? Did that person come across as happy, sad, nervous, shy, angry? I love using award shows such as the *Kids' Choice Awards* to help children assess how their peers come across and what kind of first impression they leave with an audience. If possible, record the program and play it back as you discuss how you feel about the people you're watching. Here's a fun angle: try the same exercise with the volume turned off.

As I've said, mastering conversation, like any other skill set, requires practice and repetition, until it becomes second nature. The initial awkwardness will ease and children will become more competent during their interactions with virtually anyone they meet.

4

Dialing In
on Dialing Out

*"The telephone, which interrupts
the most serious conversations and
cuts short the most weighty observations,
has a romance of its own."*

—Virginia Woolf

We've discussed several means by which we can make a first impression—face to face, on the Internet (or in another form of writing), and now via the phone. In this chapter, we will focus on making a great first impression on the phone (despite the fact that many of us own smartphones, yet rarely make calls!).

This lesson serves as a much-needed primer for how to actually talk with people on the phone, whether it is when our children call their friends' homes, when we call a restaurant or doctor's office to make a reservation or appointment, or a phone interview. Although we tend to view phone calls as somewhat less relevant these days, proper phone technique is unquestionably still a necessary skill for the every child's toolkit. Your child may or may not yet have his or her own phone, but is certainly using one in your household.

I'll be the first to say that I prefer an email or text over a phone call, but certain tasks are more effectively accomplished over the phone. It's imperative for children to be able to communicate on the telephone, not only for everyday interactions, but for emergencies too: you can't text 9-1-1.

I've talked to a lot of parents about this part of the socialsklz:-) curriculum and they always agree that learning to be courteous, professional, and kind on the phone is crucial. A phone call is often useful when a face-to-face meeting isn't possible: conveying feelings and intentions verbally is quite different from emailing or texting. Start with the basics first, and by the time you finish, you'll have put an end to abrupt telephone greetings like, "Where's David?" or the one-word answer, "What?" Again, this is a skill that isn't taught anywhere else, so it is our job as parents to equip our children with the ability to communicate on the phone. And one last note: this is a favorite lesson of kids. I received a thank-you note from my student Anjali, thanking me for teaching her the right way to phone her friends.

Five Common Problems Children Encounter When Talking on the Phone

• Mumbling or not speaking clearly (typically because the child is shy or nervous)

• Failing to introduce themselves by first and last name and forgetting to say "hello" and "goodbye"

• Asking if they "can" speak with someone instead of if they "may"

• Being unable to take a message

• Being unprepared to think on the spot and forgetting to think through the conversation ahead of time

Fun Fact: Alexander Graham Bell, who invented the telephone in 1876, believed one should answer the phone with "Hoy, Hoy"—not "Hello." The phrase

"to put someone on hold" evolved from the moment when Bell handed the phone to his assistant Mr. Watson and said, "Here, hold this."

In our classrooms, we use red phones that our students LOVE and gravitate towards, one of which is an old-school rotary phone. The "initiator" always uses that phone. While you might not have access to a rotary phone, kids love to role-play with props, so see if you can find old phones. For a creative spin, bananas will do the trick: it will make the lesson that much more fun.

The key difference between making a first impression in person and on the phone is that we can't see the person we're speaking with on the phone. Because we don't have a visual, we're required to make a first impression with our voices and the way we use our words. Explain that speaking audibly, enthusiastically, and clearly is necessary when you make and receive phone calls. In order to speak effectively, it's helpful to hold the phone properly as well.

Unless you're making a video call, the person you're calling can't see you, so children need to identify themselves. Explain that we all need to "identify" ourselves with our first and last names, just as we do when introducing ourselves in person. But as with any other first impression, coming across as a polite and genuine person is a priority too. Start by practicing "Hello, this is [First Name Last Name]." Conduct a "sound check" with children: were you able to hear them? Was what they said clear? Did they seem enthusiastic?

Now it's time to pick up your phones and learn how to speak into the receiver. Show kids where the speaker is and point out that it can't be obstructed. Be sure they're holding the phone properly, with the earpiece positioned correctly too. As they say "Hello, this is [First Name Last Name]," make sure that they aren't holding the receiver too close; demonstrate the best practice for holding a phone. I like to have fun with this, showing kids how it sounds on the other end when someone speaks (and breathes) with the receiver too close, as well as how hard it is to hear when someone isn't speaking into the receiver at all. Create a phone skills journal entry and start with a list of the most important elements of speaking on the phone.

LESSON

Because this lesson involves so much role-play and practice, I'm going to jump right into the phone scripts with the focus on the hands-on exercises. Each of the phone scripts below serves as a scenario that your children should be able to handle before making and receiving calls. If your children are already using the phone, this will serve as a very good review or lesson on how calls should be managed. These are scripts we use in the classroom, and you may want to add or edit based on your own "house rules."

In the first scenario, you're going to be the mother of "Jack" and your child is calling Jack to have a playdate. Explain to your children that when they make a call it's important to think through what they're calling about and what they will say. So, for example, if your child is asking for a playdate, it's important to have reviewed when it will be, at what time, and where. Demonstrate for your children that if you do not speak up or speak right away, the person on the other end of the line has no way of knowing who is there. Then demonstrate the correct way by immediately asking, "Hey, Jack, do you want to have a playdate?" Explain each of these scenarios with your child before picking up the phones to review the scripts.

SCENARIO 1: YOUR CHILD IS CALLING "JACK" FOR A PLAYDATE

CALLER: [dials] (ask your child make the dialing sound as they press the keys)

ANSWERER: Hello?

CALLER: Hi! This is [First Name Last Name]. May I please speak to Jack?*

Make sure to explain to your children that when you ask permission for something you use the word "may" rather than "can."

ANSWERER: Yes, just a moment please.

Answerer places the call on HOLD or MUTE to ask Jack if he wants to take the call. Explain to your children why it's important to put a caller on hold: you don't necessarily want the caller to be able to hear what you're saying.

JACK: Hello?

YOUR CHILD: Hi, Jack. This is [First Name Last Name]. I was wondering if you'd like to come over for a playdate on Sunday at 2 o'clock at our house.

JACK: That sounds great! Let me ask my [mom/dad/caretaker]. Hold on just a moment, please.

Jack asks his parent or guardian for permission.

JACK: I'd love to. I'll see you then, thanks for asking.

YOUR CHILD: Great. Can't wait to see you. Bye.

JACK: Bye.

Often children forget to say goodbye, so remind them to do so during the exercise.

SCENARIO 2: YOUR CHILD'S FRIEND CALLS ABOUT A PLAYDATE

Your child is now the receiver of the phone call and he or she is called to the phone. Use the script above, and reverse roles. When the caller asks, "May I please speak with [Your Child's Name]?" the grammatically correct response is, "Yes, this is she [or he]," not "this is her."

SCENARIO 3: YOUR CHILD IS CALLING TO INVITE "ADRIANA" FOR A PLAYDATE AND LEAVING A VOICEMAIL*

Make sure to remind your child to wait for the beep.

CALLER: Hi, this is [First Name Last Name]. I'm calling for Adriana to see if she can join me for a playdate on Sunday at 2 o'clock at our house. My telephone number is [your telephone number]. Again, that's [your telephone number].* Thanks, goodbye.

Explain that the reason for leaving the telephone number twice in a voicemail is to ensure that the person has the time to write your number down. And again, speaking clearly and slowly is extremely important during this exercise.

Before your child works on this exercise, make sure that you've discussed what the "ask" is and the number you'd like friends of your children to call back: your home phone, your cell phone, or your child's cell phone, if he or she has one. And double-check that your children know your cell phone and home phone by heart. If they don't, come up with a jingle to help them remember, and make it part of the goals in this lesson to have memorized those numbers by the end of the week. While they may have your number on speed-dial in their phones, it is possible that they may run into an emergency in which they don't have their phones. So your children MUST know the numbers at which they can reach you in case of an emergency.

SCENARIO 4: YOUR CHILD "PATRICK" CALLS AN OFFICE TO ASK FOR HIS PARENT AND GETS A RECEPTIONIST/COWORKER

RECEPTIONIST: Hello, this is [Company Name], how may I help you?

CALLER: Hi, this is Patrick Griffin, [Parent's First and Last Name's] son. [If it's important] Is he/she available to talk? It's important.

[Not so important] Is he/she free to talk?

[It can definitely wait] Could you ask him/her to call me at home when he/she has a free moment please?

The receptionist will either transfer the child to the parent's extension, let the parent know to call the child back, or ask to take a message.

If the child wants to convey a message to the parent via the receptionist:

CALLER: Could you please let him/her know that I want his/her permission to [do something/go somewhere]?

RECEPTIONIST: Absolutely.

CALLER: Okay, thank you. Bye.

RECEPTIONIST: Goodbye.

SCENARIO 5: YOUR CHILD ANSWERS THE PHONE AND CALLER ASKS TO SPEAK TO MOM, ELIZABETH

CALLER: Hi, this is [Name], may I please speak with Elizabeth Owens?

ANSWERER: Hi, [Caller's Name]. Let me find out if she is available.

Please hold on a moment.

CALLER: Sure.

Child puts the phone on hold or mute or covers the speaker to ask his or her mother if she is available to speak to the caller. If yes:

ANSWERER: [Caller's Name]? Here's Elizabeth.

CALLER: Thanks.

Elizabeth takes the phone.

SCENARIO 6: CHILD ANSWERS AND HAS TO TAKE A MESSAGE BECAUSE THE INTENDED RECIPIENT OF THE CALL IS UNAVAIL-ABLE OR NOT HOME

Ask children to take out their journals and write out a MESSAGE form with the following:

• Who the message is for

• Caller name (first and last)

• Date and time of call

• Telephone number

• Notes (asked to meet for dinner next week).

For older children, ask them what they think are the most important things to write down when taking a message.

ANSWERER: Hello?

CALLER: Hi, this is [Name], may I please speak with Olivia Greene?

ANSWERER: My mom is not available right now, but I can take a message if you'd like.*

CALLER: Thanks, that would be great. Could you please let her know that I'd like to meet up for dinner next week? She can reach me at [phone number].

ANSWERER: That's [phone number] right? (repeats phone number to caller) I will let her know. (A child should not say, "She'll call you back," or "I'll have her call you.")

CALLER: Thank you.

ANSWERER: You're welcome. Good-bye.

Explain to your kids that under no circumstances should they inform a caller that they're home alone or that their parents aren't home.

SCENARIO 7: YOUR CHILD NEEDS TO CALL 9-1-1 IN AN EMERGENCY

Review with your child what constitutes a genuine emergency. I also like to discuss with my students what they should do if they accidentally dial 9-1-1. At one point, when I worked in an office where we had to dial "9" to get an outside call, I accidentally pressed 9-1-1. When this happens it's important to stay on the line to say that it was an accidental call. 9-1-1 calls are taken very, very seriously. Law enforcement can be dispatched even for hang-ups.

ANSWERER: Hello, this is 9-1-1. What is your emergency?

CALLER: Yes, I'd like to report an accident.

Help your child understand that they need to provide complete information: who, what, when, and where, and any specific details. Explain that even if they're in a panic situation or something is really scary and they can't talk, they should stay on the line because any call, whether made from a landline or a cell phone, can be traced. For the lesson, create a mock emergency scenario and describe it to your child, and then model how to make the call to 9-1-1. Ask your child to write in his or her journal the details of *who, what, when, and where*. Try a different emergency scenario and have your child make the practice call to 9-1-1 once more.

REVIEW AND PRACTICE

Review important aspects of the lesson. If phone usage remains a challenge for your children, have them write an outline or a script before they set out to make a call.

APPLICATION AND GOALS

Make a concerted effort to initiate one phone conversation each evening with a family member or friends. Whether the conversation lasts a few minutes or an hour is beside the point. We could start a revolution and bring phone conversations back from the brink of extinction! Kick the week off on the right note with a list of who you'll call during the week: perhaps a friend, or a restaurant, an office, or a store. And make a call to someone special, like a grandparent or friend. Even with the conveniences of modern technology, a phone call "just because" is delightful to receive and is also a good place to practice conversationsklz:-).

5

Managing Friendships, Relationships, and Sticky Social Situations

"It is important to make sure your child has the best chance to succeed in the world, and a way to do this is to make sure your child is socialized for the real world. Do they know how to make friends? Do they know how to share? Can they teach their talent to others and without showing it off? Do they know how to adapt to situations as they arise? Make sure your child is prepared for the world outside of your house . . . ."

—Dr. Phil McGraw

Although parents may find it difficult to admit, each and every child is born as an egocentric being. This is not to say that all children will stay this way, but as tiny creatures who can only communicate by crying, they are born with their own survival in mind. Yet as children start to grow older and learn to survive on their own, they naturally crave human interaction. There is no question that every child wants to have friends and be considered a good friend, but often he or she doesn't get enough direction to navigate the vast intricacies of human interaction.

Making friends, maintaining friendships, and in some cases ending friendships is a rocky road, and the arts of empathy, thoughtfulness, patience, and kindness are some of the greatest skills we can help our children learn. In our modern world, kids take a longer time to learn these lessons because they have fewer siblings, less face-to-face interaction, and less unstructured play. Because these lessons aren't typically taught at school, it's our job as parents to explicitly teach our little ones. Friendship skills might seem impossible to "teach," outside of living by example, but there are basic guidelines and parameters that are vital to instill in your child. Spending time on these valuable lessons will contribute to your child's happiness and well-being in a truly remarkable way.

In the years since I founded the socialsklz:-) program, one email I received sticks in my mind as especially aggressive and negative. It was from an anonymous "tiger mom" who was outraged by a blog post I'd written about the "tiger mom" parenting style. (It's hard to take someone seriously who writes hate mail and then doesn't put a name to it, but in any case, she didn't grasp what I was trying to get across in my post on the New York City Private Schools blog.) Here's the gist of what I wrote: while I ardently believe in the hard work and perseverance in academics that the author of *Battle Hymn of the Tiger Mother*, Amy Chua, demands of her children, I believe that her parenting style diminishes the opportunity for children to learn and socialize with their peers. The "tiger" style of parenting bases the success of children wholly on performance of cognitive skills: grades, tests, and the constant practice of arithmetic, language lessons, and memorization. This particular parent reprimanded me for even questioning the success of the "tiger" style of parenting when a very high percentage of "tiger" offspring fill the seats of Ivy League institutions.

My first response is to ask, How do we define success? Is it grades and a position in college? Does that guarantee a successful life? What about children's emotional intelligence and their ability to socialize, work in groups, and communicate? It's during playdates and sleepovers (which Chua doesn't allow) that children learn these very skills: how to manage the business of human relationships and friendships, sharing, negotiating the natural hierarchy in life, and group rivalries. These valuable non-cognitive lessons bolster a child's development from a social and emotional perspective as well as their social IQ. Encouraging your kids to interact with others is so important, particularly on playdates, which expose kids to many unique and unpredictable situations that help them learn meaningful lessons. And these experiences provide the opportunity for you to guide your children in managing friendships, a skill that they will use for the rest of their lives.

Five Common Problems Children Encounter When Managing Friendships

- Unable to put themselves in someone else's shoes

- Tend to remain in their own circles

- Unable to respond to ridicule

- Cannot read body language

- Unable to extend a genuine apology

LESSON

Kids need to develop a sense of "other" so they can successfully negotiate the many social situations in which they will find themselves. By the end of this lesson your children will learn the key aspects of managing friendships.

Start out this lesson with an activity. I initially read about this activity on Facebook, and after doing a bit of research, I found that it was credited to a New York City school teacher named Paula. Thank you, Paula! Ask your children to draw a face. Allot 5 minutes to sketch and ask that they include as many details of the face as they can. Once they're finished, ask them to crumple the paper into the smallest ball they can make. Suggest that they stomp on it if they like and then ask children to unfold the paper. As they're doing so, ask them to describe how the drawing has changed. Show them how scarred and damaged the paper looks, and then explain that this is precisely what happens when another child is made fun of or ostracized. This activity exemplifies how quickly we can hurt someone; the lines or tears on the paper represent the metaphorical scars that remain there forever.

Making fun of or criticizing others is never acceptable—neither in a crowd nor in a more intimate setting. Sometimes it seems harmless to join in on the "jokes" and fun, but participating as a bystander is just as bad as hurling insults. Ask kids to imagine how they would feel if the tables were turned. What would they do? In Chapter 1 we discussed how meaningful body language is; it's important to illustrate to children just how hurtful negative body language can be. Turning your back in the midst of conversation or rolling your eyes can have negative repercussions that can be equally painful. Just like shouting at someone, it says that you don't care for or respect the person you're speaking with.

Share a story from your life about when you were made fun of, or share about someone else who was ridiculed. I still remember the girl who was picked on at my grammar school and how cruel the boys were to her, and I can recall being made fun of myself when I was in seventh grade. Sharing those stories opens up the lesson so it will feel more like a dialogue than a lecture.

Although the term "bullying" is commonly used these days, it is so overused that children seem to tune out when they even hear the term. In teaching lessons about friendships, I simply describe acts of bullying without using the term, and instead I focus on the feelings associated with it. Talking about the feelings involved also serves a dual purpose because you can talk about how it feels to be the recipient of cruel jokes while also shedding light on the role of the instigator, who could very well be your child.

Whether it is at school, during sporting events, or at home with siblings, when kids are ridiculed, there is a way to manage it. Even if your child has never been made fun of or been the butt of a joke, come up with a "game plan"—because at some stage in his or her life, it will inevitably happen. Kids who have a plan to cope with situations like these have more confidence. For example, think about the many hours that political candidates spend preparing for a debate. They work for days, weeks, and years so that they're ready with every answer for any argument or attack. As much as we want to shield our children from conflict and hurtful people, it is part of life. Acknowledging this and giving our children the tools to handle a potentially uncomfortable situation offer the best solution.

Ask your child to take out his or her journal and write down three sticky situations or instances in which he or she was made fun of or was the recipient of a hurtful joke. Here are some examples that I've heard in the classroom: "My best friend recently became best friends with someone else and now they leave me out and say mean things to me," or "My brother makes fun of me every day for the way I dress." Share with children a few of the difficult situations you've encountered in order to highlight the ways in which friendships can sometimes be painful or the instances in which people may have good intentions but can end up inadvertently hurting others. Reassure children that these situations are manageable. Ask your child to create a heading called Sticky Situations Game Plan. If you can, refer back to your child's difficult situations (and even how he or she managed them) throughout this lesson.

I always suggest that the first line of defense is to ignore the hurtful comment so that you're not giving attention to it. Paying the heckler more attention allows their bad behavior to have a bigger impact. A problematic response is to start defending yourself, which in essence makes you look insecure. One of the most effective tactics to address and put an end to mean comments is simply to move on and let it roll off your back. Responding this way will demonstrate that you can manage the situation yourself.

If the pestering persists, the next line of defense is to express your feelings and then ask the person who is bothering you to stop. Give children an example of how to address the comments. "I feel _____ when you _____."

There is no feeling that is "right" or "wrong," and feelings cannot be argued with. Practice saying "I feel _____ when you _____." I like to give kids the opportunity to first try to work out the problem themselves. If your child's request of the heckler to stop doesn't work, then I suggest that he or she speak with you or any trusted adult to get help in coping with the situation. Figure out which adults your child trusts. Don't be offended if your child chooses to talk to another adult; he or she may feel too ashamed or embarrassed to speak with you—children don't want to disappoint their parents.

Learning how to handle adversity and cope with difficult ethical situations is challenging, but it's a tremendously useful skill set. In the beginning you will serve as a guide to your children, but as they learn the skills for themselves, you'll have set your child on a path to success. Ultimately, you will take pride and joy in watching them apply those skills in real life, and they too will take pride in their new strengths.

Being a Good Friend

Now that we've covered managing adversity, we can start working with kids on the more positive aspects of friendship—how to be a good friend. There are a few common characteristics of good friends. First and foremost, people like to be around positive people. Open up journals and have kids write an entry called "A Good Friend Is. . ." Ask them to list at least five characteristics of a good friend.

In this case, "positive" means the enjoyable qualities of someone who is a good friend, despite whatever flaws they have. To put it simply, a friend is someone who is generally happy and who makes people around them feel good, someone who doesn't often complain or always talk about problems. Ask kids about people they know who are happy or pleasant, and who make them feel good. Ask your child what makes someone seem "happy." Happy people don't necessarily need to be outgoing, though many are; they can be quiet people who happen to express their happiness in more intimate settings, like smaller groups of friends or in one-on-one conversations. Ask your child if he or she knows anyone who fits the bill. It very well might be your child. Ask your child if he or she knows a "Debbie Downer" and discuss what makes the person seem that way. (Feel free to change the description to "Danny Downer" because these characteristics are gender-neutral.)

A GOOD FRIEND IS INTERESTED IN OTHERS AND ASKS QUESTIONS. Let's refer back to the conversationsklz:-) skills from Chapter 3 (page 70). I love to use the often funny example of the person who chatters incessantly about himself or herself without ever asking the other person a question. Suggest that your child ask you a question. For example, if your child asks, "How was your day?" draw on your best acting skills and babble on and on about how your day was, what you did, how great it was, how great your life is, how good you are at sports, and so on. To make sure you get your point across, speak very quickly. Kids will most likely laugh and quickly see the point: no one likes to be a spectator in a conversation. Review the key aspects of conversations: give more than one-word responses without hijacking the conversation entirely, and ask questions of your conversation partner. Refer back to Chapter 3 for a few conversation starters. This is a good time to review the timing of conversations and perhaps take out your timer as you prepare a refresher.

A GOOD FRIEND CARES ABOUT OTHERS. Caring means that we take note of our friends' lives and care about them in every way. Here is an enjoyable activity to accompany this portion of the lesson. Ask your kids to think about one or two of their friends and then review how much they know about them. Here are a few basics that kids might want to know about each of their friends: where does he or she live? Does he or she have siblings? If so, how many and how old are they? What is his or her favorite sport or hobby? What is his or her favorite food? When is his or her birthday? What is he or she really good at? Start a journal entry titled "Friend Questionnaire." Ask your children to write five questions they think they should be able to respond to about any friend. Then ask them to think of one of their friends and see if they can respond to each of the questions.

This journal entry can serve as a general guideline for what your children should know about their friends. If they don't know the responses to the questions now, ask them to find out on their own by making a phone call and using their phonesklz:-) or asking the next time they're with their friend. You might even want to do this activity, or a modified version of it, as a family; for example, you might ask your children if they know where you were born or where you grew up. Knowing these things about friends is important and can also ensure that your children are able to prepare questions that will demonstrate care toward their friends. For example, if a friend's birthday is coming up, a good question to ask is, "Are you looking forward to your birthday?" This shows a deeper level of interest and concern for someone else's well-being. Unlike the more general conversationsklz :-) that we covered in Chapter 3, these are more poignant and thoughtful questions particular to one person that really help build friendships.

A FRIEND COMPLIMENTS OTHERS. Add an entry to your Friend Questionnaire: "My friend is good at_____." Then ask your child to write a compliment based on that skill. A key to complimenting is to make it genuine and meaningful, rather than a generic, "I like your shirt." Take a moment to explain that compliments aren't necessarily about one's appearance or a fun possession. Review the skill your child particularly likes about his or her friend, and then help create a very specific compliment. For example, if the friend is thoughtful, your child can say "I love that you're really thoughtful, and it really meant a lot to me when you asked about my vacation. Thanks!"

It's amazing what a simple and genuine compliment can do. Compliments can open people up and generally make them feel good; based on my experience, kids want to make others feel good. Think about the last time someone complimented you, and how it made you feel. Work with your child to come up with compliments that feel natural. I live in a big city, and I always make a point to connect with at least three new people a day. Because my city is also home to more than eleven million people, it would be a far more pleasant place if everyone made a point to do the same: what a better place our world would be! An easy way to connect is by giving an honest compliment to someone for being extra nice, funny, or smart, for example. Here's a challenge for you and your children: on any given day, attempt to give three compliments, say "excuse me" three times, and ask three genuine or thoughtful questions.

A FRIEND TAKES NOTE OF MOODS AND EMOTIONS. Sometimes it can be challenging to read other people's moods and expressions, even for adults, but helping children to understand how to read people and their feelings is a valuable lesson. It is often quicker and more accurate to read a person's body language (a facial expression or a gesture) than it is to interpret what he or she says. Although people may claim they feel a certain way, their actions may belie that.

Body language can reveal whether someone is happy or sad, mad or playful, quiet or excited. When children learn to read the body language of the people around them, their friends will find great comfort in knowing that your child cares enough to know how they feel. Try this activity: put on a DVD—not a cartoon, but something with real-life characters. Mute the sound, and ask your kids to write down what they think each person is feeling. Then replay that scene with sound and see if the assessments are accurate. Talk about what specific body movements and facial expressions that make someone seem happy, sad, excited, angry or nervous. It's a fascinating exercise. Here is another activity: ask your children to show you, without speaking, that they really, really want the pen in your hand. Or that they don't want to go to school today. That they're sad because a friend said something really hurtful. Try acting out each scenario to emphasize how powerful body language can be.

Here's another great exercise: take the friendship scenarios from the journal and ask kids to select one and express how that situation makes them feel without saying a word. You have to determine what your child is feeling based solely on nonverbal body language.

A FRIEND IS TRUSTWORTHY. Each of us shares specific information with those whom we trust. When friends feel close they share things about themselves which make a friendship closer and often more meaningful. It's an honor to be a confidante to someone, and it takes a long time to establish that in a friendship. An important aspect of friendship is being able to keep things in confidence and to oneself. Sensitive or personal information that is shared among friends should not be shared with others. Let friends share that information if they want to and keep the information to yourself. If you break a friend's confidence, it may never be extended again. Friends don't talk about friends behind their backs—ever. Ask your children to think about how it would feel to share something private with a friend, only to have that friend share it with others.

Occasionally, though, in order to be a very good friend, a child may need to break a confidence in order to reach out to an adult for help. I can remember a tIme like that in my life. I was in the eighth grade, and my best friend was starving herself. She'd gotten down to 90 pounds, and I remember picking up the pay phone at school to call her mom to talk about it. She wound up going to a clinic to get better and was out of school for six months. Although she didn't like me for a week or two, in the long run, we saved her life. She was able to get her eating disorder under control and she and I are still very dear friends. I'm happy she is alive and thriving. Review a few instances that could merit reaching out to an adult or warrant breaching a friend's trust in order to ensure his or her safety, security, or well-being.

A FRIEND SHARES. I'm not referring to sharing a toy or a video game, although that's important too—I mean that a friend shares life. Close friends share things with each other, which creates a close bond. Friends open up by sharing their thoughts and feelings, and what makes them tick. It's important to know who we can and cannot open up to. Friendships should grow gradually, and it's likely that you'll be more emotionally intimate with the people you know the best. Talk about which people your children know the best, and who they might share their thoughts and feelings with. Trust has to be established before we can share confidential or private information or thoughts.

In life, it's important to have more than one friend. Friendships can change, we can change, others can change, and life can change. For example, someone we're close to during a given school year might not be the person we're as close to during another. When the dynamic of a friendship changes, it's okay to expand our circle of friends. That doesn't mean we can't still be friends, but sometimes we're just not as close. That's why it's important to focus on more than just one person. If we have multiple friends, it's easier on us when friendships evolve; generally speaking, the more friends, the merrier. If we do move on from a friendship, communicating can be helpful. It's never wise to end on a bad note or to make enemies.

A FRIEND APOLOGIZES. Every now and then we do things that hurt other's feelings. Often kids (and even adults) have a hard time apologizing or simply don't want to. Here is yet another valuable lesson to bestow upon your children. Explain that we must always take responsibility for our actions; occasionally, we end up hurting someone and when we do we must say "I'm sorry" if we are to make things right again with a friend (or family member). This lesson is a great forum to address apologies because often we end up telling children (especially younger ones) to apologize, which can easily result in a very half-hearted "I'm sorry."

Although it's best to apologize right away, there may be legitimate reasons to delay: sometimes a situation needs to be diffused, or a child needs time to reflect. It's important to set the tone so that children don't view apologizing as a terrible experience. It can be difficult to own shame, but ultimately it's a very cathartic experience to apologize and make amends. Go ahead and model an apology for your child. Modeling the skills from Chapter 1, stand up, make eye contact, focus, and say, "I'm sorry that I said those things about you. I know it hurt your feelings, [name], and I'm really sorry to have hurt you." Avoid adding a "but" to your "I'm sorry" because it can make you appear defensive. Your apology doesn't need to be long-winded. Think of some instances in which an apology might be necessary. Ask your child to create a journal entry called "Apologies," and enter a sample apology. Rehearsing an apology is never a bad idea, particularly with a child who has a hard time saying, "I'm sorry." Here is the bottom line: we all make mistakes, but we need to own them, apologize, and learn from them.

◖◖ REVIEW AND PRACTICE ◗◗

Review some traits that go into being a good friend and ask kids if they're a good friend to others. Ask kids to evaluate whether their closest friends meet their criteria of a good friend. Review how body language can express more than words can and also review a genuine apology. If you're up for it, take the DVD exercise and act it out in real life. Keep it simple: sigh, shrug, and look down, to express disappointment. See if your child can guess what emotion you're feeling. Then repeat the same action but add words—in this example, you might say something like, "Oh no, it's bedtime already?"

⟨⟨ GOALS AND APPLICATIONS ⟩⟩

Challenge kids to give three compliments a day for a one-week period and to ask each of their close friends a very specific question about their hobbies, interests, or an event in their lives. Ask kids to make a point to expand the friendship circle and engage someone new this week. Ask your children to reflect on whether they owe an apology to anyone; if they believe they do, then work on phrasing the apology with them. You may want to add a few of your own specific practice exercises based on your child's needs. This is the right time to do that, rather than in the moment when a complex social situation arises.

6

Gratitude, Attitude, and Everyday Thoughtfulness

"Showing gratitude is one of the simplest yet most powerful things humans can do for each other."

—Randy Pausch

Some time ago, I was watching ABC News and happened upon an interview with Randy Pausch. He was a college professor at Carnegie Mellon University who was diagnosed with terminal pancreatic cancer in 2006 and was told he had three to six months to live. On September 18, 2007, he taught one last class entitled, "The Last Lecture: Really Achieving Your Childhood Dreams," which became a *New York Times* bestselling book and can still be seen today on YouTube. Among the priceless lessons that are included in Pausch's lecture is one that is incredibly simple, yet powerful: we must be grateful. Imagine a man who is reflecting on his life in the face of death and who chooses to talk about the value of gratitude.[1] This was a striking reminder to me that we all have something to be grateful for.

When I founded socialsklz:-) and developed the various components of each workshop, I decided to include a lesson called "Gratitude: The Value of Everyday Thoughtfulness." To this day it remains an essential part of our workshop series. I included this lesson in the socialsklz:-) toolkit because I recognized how much gratitude and thoughtfulness have enhanced many of my relationships with friends, teachers, family, and my husband. I regularly incorporate these traits into my daily living, and this has helped me be a more empathetic human being. Expressing gratitude is effective; it's rewarding for all parties involved, and it feels good to acknowledge what we're grateful for. Taking the time to recognize the efforts of others and to convey genuine thanks and appreciation makes other people feel special, which in turn makes us feel good. Simply put, it's good karma. When we're good to others, they're (mostly) good to us in return.

Numerous studies on gratitude support the way it is linked to happiness, well-being, and stronger relationships with others. A 2003 study at the University of California-Davis showed that "a daily gratitude intervention (self-guided exercises) with young adults resulted in higher reported levels of the positive states of alertness, enthusiasm, determination, attentiveness, and energy, compared to a focus on hassles or a downward social comparison (ways in which participants thought they were better off than others)."[2] Another study concluded that "children who practice grateful thinking have more positive attitudes toward school and their families."[3]

Apart from our programming them to say "please" and "thank you," children need some help in understanding why they're professing thanks: if we are to live in a state of gratitude, we need to be aware. Although it's not an inherent character trait in any young child, gratitude can be taught, and the good feelings that come from being grateful will encourage children to continue to think of others, rather than only of themselves. Kids who don't learn to be thankful can often be viewed as entitled or selfish. The practice of being grateful helps children become more loving, appreciative, compassionate, and sensitive to the feelings of others. It's for this reason that I have paired gratitude and attitude in this chapter. The relationship between the two is cyclical—people with positive attitudes tend to be grateful people, and people who express gratitude tend to have positive attitudes. Instilling gratitude in your child now will surely benefit him or her later in life too. The University of California-Davis study I referenced earlier also showed that grateful people report higher levels of happiness and optimism—along with lower levels of depression and stress.[4]

5 Common Problems Children Have in Understanding Gratitude, Attitude, and Thoughtfulness

- **Unaware of the importance of gratitude and thoughtfulness in everyday life**
- **Tend to focus on what they want rather than what they have**
- **Believe that people "should" do things for them**
- **Inclined to put themselves first**
- **Have difficulty expressing gratitude in meaningful ways**

LESSON

Let's turn up the gratitude needle: Ask children to open their journals to the next blank page. They can call this journal entry "Gratitude: It's

Party Time!" I frame this lesson in the context of a mock birthday party, which is always a big hit with kids. It's a great lesson in "please" and "thank you" gratitude, and much more. If you have the resources, try using props like party hats, gift bags or paper bags, thank-you notes or any type of stationery, and some type of party treat like cupcakes. It's up to you as to how far you want to take the party theme.

The idea here is that gratitude and attitude are woven into the party, one of the ideal places in which gratitude should be in full-force (and we'll cover a few other lessons during this activity, too). Before getting started with the party, ask your children what gratitude means to them, and ask them to write in their journals what they are grateful for. They may initially write about material possessions so be sure to give a few examples such as acts of kindness, love, and care.

There are seven components to the party. Ask kids to write them down (remind them to leave space for notes):

1. **Host preparation: invitations**

2. **Guest preparation: gifts and cards**

3. **Party time!**

4. **Gift-giving and receiving**

5. Snack time

6. Thank-you notes

7. Closing

As you review the various components, prompt kids to journal about the important aspects of each element.

Invitations

Explain to children that this is a mock party, so you're going to practice making all the necessary arrangements in advance, including invitations. Take out some paper and review the important details an invitation must cover: type of party, date, time, address, RSVP, and relevant contact information. You can also take this opportunity to explain the meaning of "RSVP." It's an acronym for a French phrase: "*Répondez s'il vous plâit*," or in English, "Respond, please." Take a moment to go over the difference between RSVP and "Regrets Only"; let children decide which they prefer to use on their own invitations. Be sure that invites don't say "Please RSVP," since the "please" is redundant: the SVP in RSVP stands for "please" in French. Explain that invitations should be sent out at least two weeks in advance of the event, and even further in advance if the event is larger.

I often share with my students an experience I had a year ago when I sent out an email invitation for a party to about 50 friends four weeks ahead of the date. I forgot to include an "RSVP By" date, and only received eight confirmations and four regrets. On the day of the party, I received a flurry of text messages and wound up with three times the number of guests than I had expected! Fortunately, I was able to order more food and beverages to accommodate the rest of my guests, but I was cutting it close. Afterward, I realized two important components of the invitation: the host should make sure to include an RSVP, and the guests should respond to the invitation in a timely fashion. Ask kids what problems could arise when guests aren't responsive and the host doesn't know what kind of crowd to expect.

Take a moment to discuss how to deliver the invitations. A good rule of thumb is that if you are inviting friends from school, invitations should only be distributed in class if every single child is invited. If not, the invitations should be mailed to avoid hurt feelings. It's a terrible feeling to realize that you've been left out as invitations are being distributed to a select group of people. It's downright hurtful, and it's very inconsiderate of the party host. Another option is to simply create an e-invitation through one of many online options; if the guest list is limited, this is a good option because it is discreet. While many etiquette gurus will say that formal mailed invitations are the only option, sending evites is environmentally friendly, saves time, and can make it remarkably easy to manage RSVPs. I tend to send mailed invitations if the occasion is particularly special, like a wedding or my daughter's first birthday (but future parties will be e-invitations!).

Gifts and Cards

Ask kids to take out a piece of paper or a notecard and draw a picture of a present for you or another person in the group (a stuffed animal, sneakers, a video game). I like to use notecards because they fit nicely into boxes or party bags. Review a budget for a friend's birthday gift and decide on what items might fit in that price range. After you're done drawing the gifts, ask kids to put the notecards into gift bags or brown paper bags. If you have time and want an arts-and-crafts project, you can ask kids to wrap the gifts. (Wrapping a present is a nice skill to put in the toolkit for life!) These will serve as presents for the birthday boy or girl.

We've all received generic store-bought cards with a pre-printed message and the sender's signature. A card on any occasion is thoughtful, but taking the time to personalize it with a handwritten note, or even making the card, means that you went the extra mile to make the gift more thoughtful. Ask children to make their own cards to accompany the "gift" and talk about how special it is to receive a handwritten personal message with the gift. If the gift were for a friend, a note might read something like, "Dear Tom, Thanks for being such a dear friend to me, especially when I am having a tough day. Happy Birthday!" After writing a personalized note, talk through appropriate closings, such as "Warmly," "Yours Truly," "Love," or other options. Since the card identifies the giver of the gift, make sure it stays with the gift and is visible.

Party Time!

Now that we're all set with invitations, cards, and party hats, decide on a guest of honor; take turns if you're working with more than one child. One can play "guest" while the other plays "birthday girl/boy," or you can play one of the roles.

Begin as if it were a real party: guests should ring the doorbell or knock on the door. In advance of guests' arrival, review Chapter 1, page 26, for proper greetings. Review the protocol for arrival: First, greet the guests. Set the scene—ask your child to go out the front door of your home with their "gift." You're the parent, and he or she is the guest. Ask your child to hold the gift in her left hand, freeing the right to shake hands. Your child should introduce herself, thank the parent for the kind invitation, and shake hands. Next she should greet the guest of honor with "Happy Birthday! Thank you for having me," and give the child the gift. Sometimes you'll need to wait patiently for your turn to greet, but don't skip it. The party boy or girl should say, "Thank you so much for coming!" Using names during that quick interaction is even better; for example, "Thank you so much for coming, Gabe!" Guests should greet each other at the party, not necessarily with a handshake, but with a cordial "Hi, Faye, great to see you," or with people they've never met, "Hi my name is Faye, it's nice to meet you."

Gift-Giving and Receiving

During this part of the party, I like to create an environment separate from the work table: lay a colorful blanket on the floor and place gifts in the center. At some point, I ask the designated party boy or girl to take a seat on the blanket and give him or her a party hat or birthday crown, if you have one. If you have enough, pass out party hats to all of the guests, too. If there are a few kids at the "party," they should all have made drawings of birthday gifts for the party child. The birthday host then chooses gifts to open.

During this part of the lesson, explain to kids that they should open cards first and acknowledge the gift-giver with eye contact before opening the present. As the gift is opened, explain that they should react enthusiastically (demonstrate how you'd be enthusiastic and gracious about a present). Also, ask them what they should do if the gift is something they already have or if it's something they don't particularly like. Once the gift is open, ask the birthday party boy or girl to make eye contact again and say, "Thank you very much for the _____." In a more intimate setting with family or close friends, explain that giving a hug can be thoughtful, too. Take a moment to review who might be appropriate to hug. With the older children, ask that they also say something more specific than just "thank you." For example, if they receive a shirt, "This is great for school, I really appreciate it," or if it's a video game, "I've been dying to try this out, wow!"

The idea is that they acknowledge the gift and gift-giver with eye contact and a smile, and express sincere gratitude for the effort that someone has taken in purchasing the gift (and writing the card), in addition to the gift itself. Gift-opening isn't something to rush through: it's important to acknowledge the thought and time that the giver put into the present. The gift-giver should respond by making eye contact and saying, "You're welcome." If multiple children are participating, everyone should get a turn at playing birthday host and guest.

Snack Time

Now it's the time to enjoy a birthday treat. You can decide what the treat should be—cupcakes, or your child's favorite snack. If you have time, plan an afternoon to make cupcakes or cookies in advance; the baking activity will only add to the anticipation of the lesson. If you decide to use birthday candles, you can rotate who plays guest and birthday child so that everyone gets the opportunity to blow out some candles; or if you prefer, just skip the candles. Ask everyone to sing a quick version of "Happy Birthday," and once the candles are blown out, the host might express thanks to everyone for coming.

Kids shouldn't begin eating until everyone gets a treat; they should wait for the host to take the first bite. As the treats are given out, make sure each child makes eye contact with whomever is passing out the snacks and says, "thank you." Enjoy the snack while discussing how the party will end, and what the host and the guests will say as they leave.

Thinking and writing about gratitude calls to mind many great quotations about the topic, but I've managed to narrow it down to the following four. Take a moment or two to share a couple of them with your kids while you eat.

"Be thankful for what you have; you'll end up having more. If you concentrate on what you don't have, you will never, ever have enough."

—Oprah Winfrey

"As we express our gratitude, we must never forget that the highest appreciation is not to utter words, but to live by them."

—John F. Kennedy

"Gratitude is riches. Complaint is poverty."

—Doris Day

"Every day, think as you wake up, today I am fortunate to be alive, I have a precious human life, I am not going to waste it. I am going to use all my energies to develop myself, to expand my heart out to others; to achieve enlightenment for the benefit of all beings. I am going to have kind thoughts towards others, I am not going to get angry or think badly about others. I am going to benefit others as much as I can."

—Dalai Lama

Thank-You Notes

While they're enjoying their snacks, ask your children if they've ever given a gift and not received a thank you—or perhaps they've seen you give a gift without receiving any thanks. Share a story about a time in your life when you took the time to purchase or make a meaningful gift for someone, wrapped it, maybe even mailed it, and then never heard anything from the person who received it. The practice of thanking people is something I cannot stress enough because it's easy to do and can mean so much. Ask children how much time someone might have spent in putting together the gift for him or her. Take a tenth of that time and spend it on the thank-you note.

Here are a few occasions for which your children may want to send a thank-you note: hosting us for the weekend, visiting us if we are sick, and taking us out to dinner after a play date. I'm astounded by how few thank-you notes or emails I've received after interviewing job candidates here at social-sklz. This year, I conducted an interview with a lovely individual whom I liked a great deal, but who never bothered to be in touch afterwards. What that says to me is that this person doesn't have the drive that I'm looking for. How unfortunate that this person was apparently never taught to be grateful. Expressing gratitude in professional settings can mean a great deal, and if a hiring manager is on the fence between two candidates, a thank-you note or email can mean getting the job (or not).

During our tweenz workshops we actually write thank-you notes to the President, which is another option for you to try with your children at home. We express thanks for all the things he does for our country. Our gratitude has nothing to do with politics: anyone can see that the presidency is a difficult position, and as citizens, we can be grateful that our leader works so hard. We've now received quite a few responses from the President in the form of letters. If you do choose to write, the address is 1600 Pennsylvania Avenue, Washington, DC 20500.

Before concluding this lesson, take the time to chat with your children about the fact that gratitude is part of life. Having an attitude of gratitude comes back full circle. People are more inclined to act in kind ways toward those who exude gratitude and positivity. Gratitude should be incorporated into every single thing we do; it is not something we express only to people who are important to us; we should be in the habit of showing gratitude to anyone who shows us kindness, however small. Whether it is a best friend or a server at a restaurant, a crossing guard who guides us across the street, the cashier at the grocery store, or a family member who does something thoughtful, everyone should be thanked. Gratitude is not for special occasions only. Talk about the obvious things we show gratitude for, such as receiving presents at birthday parties, for holidays, and for other special occasions. Next, talk about the less obvious things for which we can show gratitude: it's not just for presents. A few examples might include bedtime stories, homemade dinners, and family movie night. Tell your children about something you're grateful for, and ask what they are grateful for (excluding material possessions).

Closing

Take a moment to talk about departing a party, collecting all personal belongings, and the importance of saying good-bye rather than doing a disappearing act. You employ the same skills in a proper good-bye as you do in a greeting: children can thank their hosts again. Sometimes students ask me why they need to say thank you again if they said it when they arrived. I say, "You can't thank people too many times." In my own life, I like to either email or call a party host the next day to express gratitude and to mention something specific that I loved about the party. A host often puts a great deal of effort into a party, and there is nothing nicer than a compliment after the fact.

⟪ REVIEW AND PRACTICE⟫

Take the time to go over the key aspects of a successful birthday from the point of view of both host and guest. Add a few notes to the journal as you review the lesson with kids, focusing in particular on areas they might improve on. Here is an exercise we do in every socialkidz:-) workshop series: ask your child to write a thank-you note to you, another family member, or anyone else who is special to him or her, just for being thoughtful. For example, during our workshops, students write notes to their parents like, "Dear Mom, Thank you for loving me every day and for giving me so many hugs. I love you! Love, Suzy." Kids are often focused on giving thanks for presents, so you need to really work through this exercise to stress the concept of what non-material things we can be grateful for. When we're finished writing, we mail our notes as a surprise for the recipient (if the child prefers, he or she can simply hand the note to the recipient). Mailing the note is a great exercise: kids need to know how to address envelopes properly, where to put stamps, and why a return address is crucial. For fun, ask your children if they happen to know how much a stamp costs.

I cannot say it enough: gratitude is an essential part of a happy life and living with appreciation each and every day truly improves the quality of our lives. Explain to your children that this is a lesson that can start small: from thanking someone for holding the door, to thinking about the little things that Mommy and Daddy do, like reading books, singing a song together, or even picking you up from school so you don't have to walk home. With this foundation, children will eventually learn that the most important form of thankfulness is for the things we do to make each other happy, rather than for the things we buy. Gratitude is a lesson that we can all use a refresher on, no matter how young or old we are, because let's face it—it's easy sometimes to lose track of what really matters, so the earlier children are taught this lesson, the better. And while you're at it, ask kids if they enjoyed the lesson and how they might show gratitude for it. It might be by saying "thank you," but they might also show some gratitude by helping to tidy up! As with anything in this book, don't expect a sense of gratitude to develop overnight. It will come with time as you make it part of your family culture.

◆ GOALS AND APPLICATIONS ◆

Make this the "week of gratitude." It's easy to incorporate this activity into your evening routine, perhaps over dinner. Take turns sharing things you appreciated during your day. I love doing "acts of kindness" over a week with little thoughtful deeds. When I was a little girl, my father often traveled on business trips. On some of those occasions, I'd sneak into his room before he left to put all sorts of secret notes in the pockets of his clothes, in his toiletry bag, and wherever else I could hide them. I'd be so excited for him to call from the trip and tell me that he'd found them.

You might want to consider a volunteer activity with your children this week. The exercise of moving out of our own circles and taking time to reflect on the many things we do have is time well spent. There are so many ways in which you can practice and instill thoughtfulness that don't require money, much time, or resources. Come up with a few ideas with your kids. This week, really put the theme of "living in a state of gratitude and thoughtfulness" to work in yourself as well. As you lead by example, thank the person who prepares your coffee and say something nice, and reinforce your child's efforts as you see them. I'd love to know if you see any movement on the gratitude and thoughtfulness needle!

7

Dining Intervention:
Taming the Tiger
at the Table

*"The world was my oyster,
but I used the wrong fork."*

— Oscar Wilde

Good dining skills are important throughout a child's life because eating and socializing are intertwined with our culture. As an adult, even I have to be cognizant of which fork I'm supposed to use for a particular course, so it's no surprise that I get countless calls from parents who are horrified and embarrassed by their children's table manners. You may or may not be in such an extreme position, but having a child who is well-adapted at the table is a great pleasure for everyone. And there's no question that a child who can independently manage himself or herself well at mealtimes makes us parents proud and our children proud too (even though they might not admit that to you). As the parents who call and plead with us to get their child into one of our table manners classes know all too well, it can seem like a reflection on our parenting if our children are slobs at the table, as if they have never eaten a civilized meal before. For reasons that can be generational, age-related, or a mixture of the two, grandparents view children's table manners as even more important; how well children comport themselves at the table can be a determining factor in whether they see their grandchildren as respectful young adults or boorish scoundrels.

The numerous etiquette tomes out there feature all sorts of rules, and some of these books are just downright outdated. Here are just a few of the rules I've found in various books: When someone comes to the table, a man or boy always rises to his feet and remains standing while the other person is taking his or her seat; only a man may do the ordering and may summon the wait staff; for ladies, purses belong on a stool adjacent to the table; before you even touch your napkin, wait to see if the hostess plans to say a blessing. As we all know, these days most restaurants don't offer stools for handbags (let alone chairs that have suitable backs for bag-hanging), women would be offended if a man did all the ordering, and blessings are very personal, depending entirely on religious beliefs (or lack thereof), and can been seen as offensive to others. The different sections of the "entertaining" chapter in one of the books I read features "The Formal Seated Dinner With a Staff" and "The Informal Seated Dinner Without a Maid." I can only imagine how meals with my nine-month-old would be categorized . . . without a maid, of course!

In this chapter, I've taken the old-world table manners guides and injected a good dose of the modern world in order to provide you and your children with an everyday (and democratic) toolkit of mealtime dos and don'ts, table settings, and utensil management, along with a few other tips that are simple and easy to remember.

5 Common Problems Kids Have at the Table

- **Inability to focus on anything aside from the food in front of them**
- **Not remembering how to properly set the table**

- **Eating and chewing with their mouths open**

- **Managing utensils effectively**

- **A desire to "dine and dash"**

By the end of this chapter, your "little tigers" should be able to mesmerize dinner guests with their table-setting prowess, wow waiters and waitresses with their impeccable utensil use, and make eloquent toasts like mini maids-of-honor and bite-size best men. They will see that diningsklz:-) are in fact valuable, fun, and are sometimes even rewarded. They will quickly learn what to talk about (and what not to talk about) at the table, because these are skills you can practice as a family at any (or every) meal. These new skills will be applied throughout their lives, because your children need to eat plenty of healthy meals to grow into strong young ladies and gentlemen. And I promise you, although they might roll their eyes at the very thought of "table manners," they'll appreciate them when they go out to their first dinner date or work lunch and feel confident dining in a more formal environment. You can also reassure children that these skills will take time to master, but that they will have the opportunity to practice their newfound diningsklz:-) at every meal. In fact, consider yourself forewarned: you may have your own "table manners police" on your hands after this lesson. *Bon appétit!*

I suggest beginning this activity in the kitchen or wherever you have a table and table settings available. Don't try this lesson (yet) in a restaurant, by any means. It's meant to be unintimidating, interactive, and rife with the sna-fus commonly associated with dining. We at socialsklz :-) have partnered with Alex Von Bidder, co-owner of the Four Seasons Restaurant in New York (and author of *Wiggins Learns His Manners at the Four Seasons Restaurant*). We con-duct our lessons on one of their slowest nights, before the restaurant gets busy. We teach the lesson first and by the time other dinner patrons have arrived, kids are ready to show off their new skills. So begin teaching din-ingsklz:-) from the comfort of your own dinner table and then when the kids are ready, you can take them to their favorite restaurant to amaze their fellow diners with their superb table manners!

Start by reviewing with your children the elements of a table setting: nap-kin, cups, meal plate, bread plate, and utensils (knife, spoon, forks, and if you want to get a bit more advanced, include the butter knife, dessert spoon, and appetizer fork). Other items include salt and pepper shakers and perhaps a bread basket. Feel free to include candles and anything else that your family enjoys at mealtime, to make the lesson a little more "special."

At this point, take out journals and markers and ask children to start a din-ingsklz:-) entry. We'll start by drawing a proper place setting. Draw a large plate in the center, which we'll call a meal plate. Put a large "M" on that plate. In the upper left of the drawing, draw a smaller plate with a "B" in the center—this is the bread plate. Water glasses are placed on the upper right of the meal plate—draw another circle with the letter "W." You'll see that from left to right we have the letters "B M W." Although not every child knows what a BMW is, it's a simple way to remember which side the bread plate is on and which side the water glass and other drinks are on. For those who haven't heard of BMWs, you can simply remember that the letters are in alphabetical order from left to right. This is a great trick to remember, even for us adults: we've all been at a special event and felt unsure of which plate is which on a crowded table. You can also illustrate the correct placement by joining the pointer finger and thumb of your left hand in a circle, with the other three fingers extended; you have formed the lowercase letter "b" for bread plate. With your right hand, form a lowercase letter "d" for drink.

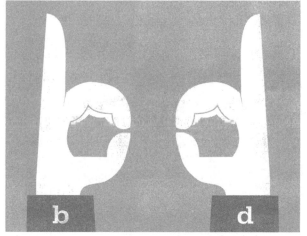

Next up are the utensils. Ask children how many letters are in the word "fork" and how many letters are in the word "left." Yes, coincidentally they both have four letters. So forks go on the left side of the plate. Now how many letters does "knife" have? And how many letters does "right" have? And "spoon?"

"Right," "knife," and "spoon" all have five letters each. So knives and spoons both go to the right of the plate, with the knife blade facing the plate. The spoon goes next to the knife. Keep in mind that if there is a spoon at the place setting, it's very likely that soup will be served. Soup is one of the few foods that one should eat with a spoon; much to your children's disbelief, it is used neither for peas nor for mashed potatoes; the fork is the proper utensil for both of those foods.

While there are all sorts of fun things that restaurants do with napkins—swans in the center of plates or fans placed in glasses—the most "proper" spot is to the left of the plate under the forks.

For those who are a bit more advanced, you can also include at the place setting a wine glass, perhaps for a "fancy" beverage. Place a dessert fork and spoon horizontally above the meal plate. Although it's more common to see dessert utensils brought out with dessert, this is the most "proper" of settings, according to etiquette gurus. A linen tablecloth or special placemats on the table might add to the fun.

Discuss the importance of setting the table neatly for a special meal, with utensils aligned closely together at the same distance from the bottom edge of the table. I suggest that kids use their pointer fingers as a guide. All plates and utensils should be one knuckle's length away from the bottom edge of the table. Organization is just as important at the table as it is in other aspects of life. It's just like a first impression, in a way. When someone takes the time to prepare a delicious meal, a proper place setting shows respect for his or her hard work, and helps each person enjoy the meal more.

Ask children to close their journals. Now they need to go ahead and set the table properly. Request that they find all items themselves: this is a good exercise to ensure that kids know where things are kept in the kitchen too. After all, these are budding "table setters" in your household who need to be in the know. Daily table setting is a great responsibility for every child.

Once the table is set, check the settings, make suggestions, and be sure the blades of knives are pointing toward plates (the direction of the knife blade is the most easily forgotten rule). Ask children to sit back down in front of their place settings to discuss utensil management.

The two main styles of eating with a knife and fork—"European" and "American"—are most easily distinguished by the way the utensils are held. In the European style, the utensils never switch hands. The fork always remains in the left hand and the knife in the right hand. The prongs of the fork are always facing downward as well, whether the fork is resting on the plate or in your hand. The tricky part of European style is how you get items like peas and rice onto a fork with the prongs facing downward. It's easiest to deploy a larger piece of meat or vegetable to form a shelf, and then push a few the smaller food items onto the larger one before bringing the fork to your mouth.

In the American or "zig-zag" style, the dominant movement is with the right hand, which holds the fork, prongs facing upward; when the knife is needed for cutting, the diner switches the fork to the left hand. The fork then serves to stabilize the food that is about to be cut, with the prongs facing downward. The knife is in the right hand, and the diner cuts above the fork, never below the fork. Once the food is cut, the diner switches utensils again, using the fork to pick up the food, prongs facing upward.

Whichever eating style you and your children prefer, it's forbidden to use the utensils as pointing tools or props for gesturing. And when you're taking a break from your plate or are finished eating, use the "resting" position or the "finished"

position for your utensils. To indicate that you are not yet finished
eating, imagine your plate as a
clock face: place the fork between
the 4 and the 5 with the prongs
facing downward, and place the
knife between the 7 and the 8,
with the blade facing inward.

When you are finished eating, place your fork and knife on
the plate at the 4 o'clock position, fork tines up and knife
blade facing the fork.

Now for the dos and don'ts
portion of the lesson. It's fun to go
over what's inappropriate at the

table: I've found that kids enjoy sharing egregious mealtime don'ts. Here are some
you might want to review: talking with your mouth full, waving utensils like a con-
ductor baton as you speak, elbows on the table, hands on your face, and slouchy
or disengaged body language. Be sure you've covered them all. Most kids know
more of the don'ts than the dos because they are corrected for their table

manners more often than they are complimented. With any luck, once you have finished the lesson the reverse will be true, and they'll forget all about their former days as champions of mashed-potato-flinging. Here are just a few mealtime dos and don'ts.

Before hosting or attending a dinner party, it's important to be nicely groomed. When I host the diningsklz :-) portion of our workshops, kids get dressed up for a party that will allow them to show off their newly acquired skills. The boys wear button-downs, hats, and an optional spray of cologne, and girls wear fun accessories, shoes, dresses, and perfume. We review attire that is inappropriate for dining (other than at a fast food restaurant): for example, no sweatpants or T-shirts. We discuss bathing, brushing teeth and hair, and taking care of fingernails. We always provide hats for the boys as a reminder that they need to be removed at the table. If your children carry mobile devices, be sure to point out that they are never to be placed on the table and that they should be turned off—not just on vibrate, but off (this is a good reminder for adults, too!). For kids, the only exception is if they're dining out with others and a parent might need to reach them. If necessary, phones can be placed on vibrate in a back pocket, but shouldn't be on the table itself. A word about coats: if your son happens to be at dinner with a lady, it's very polite to offer assistance in taking off or putting on her jacket. Although chivalry has changed in our modern world, it's not dead. You can visit our website to see our students on *The Today Show*: they were delighted by the opportunity to dress up and show off!

When dining with others, body language is important: Your body should be facing the table, not sideways. Feet should be on the floor or as close to it as you can get, with your back straight against the chair. If you're sitting at a bench, make sure your back is straight. Elbows never belong on the table, though you can rest your wrists on the edge of the table. Under no circumstances should your hands be anywhere near your face; in fact, your hands should remain above the table for the majority of the meal. If during the meal, a diner needs to use the facilities, a simple "excuse me" will do. No need to offer up the details of where you're headed: that's just "TMI." And on the topic of getting up mid-meal, I've polled many fine ladies about whether they appreciate a male dining companion's gesture of rising when they leave the table: I'd say 95 percent of women are touched when a gentleman gets up when they do. A man doesn't need to walk around the table to pull out a lady's chair; I suggest a "half" stand. But if you're on a date, gentlemen would do well to use the additional formality of pulling out a chair for a female companion as she arrives at the table: young and older ladies agree.

After we get settled at the table, we move on to how to handle the meal itself. Once food makes it to your mouth, it is to remain in your mouth, with your mouth sealed shut. Absolutely no one wants to see half-chewed food as it is in the process of being digested. What if someone asks you a question while you're chewing? Make eye contact and raise your index finger to indicate that you're chewing. Whatever you do, be sure to acknowledge the question. This is a good reason to take only manageable bites of food at any given time. The purpose of dining together is to socialize and converse. If you take small, judicious bites, you'll always be able to swallow and speak if asked a question and you'll never be tempted to talk with food in your mouth.

Sip a beverage throughout the meal; never gulp down a beverage with a big "AHHHH" when you're finished. Slurping and bubble-blowing through a straw are very strongly discouraged. Beverages shouldn't be used to wash down food already in the mouth. Remind children to chew and swallow, and then take a drink.

If you're at a restaurant without a formal host, it's proper to place the napkin on your lap as soon as you're seated. When you're at someone's home for dinner, it's customary to wait until your host puts the napkin in his or her lap and then you can do the same. A good rule of thumb is to wipe your mouth in between courses. Remind your children to wipe their mouth not with a sweeping motion, but with a delicate dabbing motion. In fact, you may want to call it an "in-between course dab." At the culmination of a meal, the napkin should be placed to the left of the plate, unfolded, but not crumpled in a ball either. It shouldn't be put back on the plate. And if your child needs to leave the table during the meal, the napkin goes on his or her chair.

Utensils should be used for anything and everything on the meal plate. In a formal dinner setting, the only thing you can eat with your fingers is the bread. Rather than cutting a dinner roll in half and buttering the entire thing or eating it all at once, diners should break off and butter each bite as it's eaten. Also, there should be no "lollipopping," as I say in class. A fork should not be used like a lollipop stick, to spear a chunk of food that you then lick or nibble. Any food that you pick up with the fork must be cut to size to fit into your mouth.

There are certain everyday dining situations—at your own home, for example—in which you can eat with your hands. Such foods as pizza, hamburgers, chicken fingers, French fries, and some sandwiches don't require utensils. For any questionable foods, first assess where you are dining. If it's on the formal side, when in doubt, just use your utensils. In a more formal Italian restaurant you might use a knife and fork for the pizza. But in a more casual setting, at a pizza parlor, utensils aren't required.

Here is a simple rule that applies to passing the salt and pepper: even if someone just asks for the salt, both salt and pepper shakers are to be passed together as a pair and should always stay together at the table.

As for the art of mealtime conversation, keep in mind that meals are intended to be enhanced by conversation. If you feel shy about eating with others, prepare a few appropriate conversation topics: you can list a few in your journal. Don't forget to review the conversationsklz:-) from Chapter 3 (page 70). Mealtime is the ideal opportunity for kids to practice initiating and maintaining a dialogue. And of course, if you're at the home of the person who cooked the meal, a compliment and expression of gratitude is in order: not just "Thanks for the great meal," but something specific. "I love how you prepared the salmon: it's cooked perfectly."

Special notes: If you have food allergies, it's important to let the host know in advance so that he or she doesn't spend the day cooking only to find out that you can't eat what was prepared. Avoid offering up a list of dozens of things you don't eat: try to give the host an idea of what things you CAN eat from the planned menu. You might say something like: "I don't eat meat, but I'll be fine with whatever sides you serve." Limit the food allergy conversation during the meal, though.

We've all had a mishap at the table. A piece of food goes flying out of your mouth, you drop food in your lap, a burp slips out, or you spill a glass of orange juice on the table. First and foremost, apologize. An accident is easily smoothed over with a meaningful "I'm so sorry about that" or an "Excuse me, please." But it isn't necessary to belabor the incident. Once the apology is made, move on. If you happen to bite into something foreign during the meal and feel the need to remove it from your mouth, pick up the napkin, turn away from the table, and place the item directly into the napkin from your mouth. An "excuse me" is appropriate here, too. Etiquette books have many different ways of handling such a situation, but this is by far the most discreet and polite.

Gifts for a Host

We typically bring something to a dinner party—a gift or an addition to the meal. You might want to review what's appropriate to bring. Sometimes children will suggest things like "a fish" or "a whole chicken," but we talk about how the host generally provides the main dish. It's good to communicate with the host in advance and to offer to bring something specific, like a side dish or a dessert. If the host says that it's not necessary to bring anything and that the meal is already planned, try bringing a simple host gift as thanks for the invitation. Here are some suggestions: a candle, a beverage, or a treat that the host can enjoy after the party, like chocolates. Of course, remember to include a note!

With children who are more advanced, a toast is a fun concept to incorporate into the lesson. In advance of making a toast it's important to prepare what you'll say. You can either rehearse mentally, or for a more important toast, write down your thoughts. At the end of a toast, guests gently clink glasses, make eye contact (this is extremely important), and offer some type of "cheers." When there are many guests, sometimes it's impossible to clink glasses with everyone at the table, but you can just lift your glass and make eye contact. Don't forget to take a sip after the toast!

Fun fact: Do you know where the word "toast" comes from? It comes from the Roman practice of dropping a piece of burnt bread into the wine to temper some of the bad wines the Romans sometimes had to drink. The charred bread actually reduced the acidity of slightly off-wines, making them more palatable.[1]

REVIEW AND PRACTICE

Here's where the fun really begins. Choose a night to have a "dinner party." Create a menu with kids and let them use their phone skills to make calls or even send out handmade invitations to see if guests can attend. This exercise offers practice in making invitations, so even if it's just immediate family, ask children to make calls or mail invitations. Let children really take charge: this is all about the lesson, so let them do as much as they can. For example, they can make up the menu and set the table, adding a few of their own special touches to the affair, and then play "host" to guests. Even some of the adult guests may not be familiar with the roles of host and guest, but don't let that stop your children from being good hosts.

Reminder: At the end of a dinner party there is nothing like getting a thank-you note or an email attesting to the great time you had and thanking the host for a few specifics of the evening. A lot of work goes into a dinner party and it's only polite to respond graciously and quickly. If you thank your child for being an excellent host, it sets a good example for them for the future, when they are playing the role of guest.

ꙮ GOALS AND APPLICATIONS ꙮ

The ultimate goal of this lesson is to instill in your children good dining skills that will last a lifetime. The constructive environment we provide in this lesson gives them the knowledge and the tools to dine in any situation with ease. The added benefit is that your children can reinforce these skills when they dine at home. You might institute a once a week dinner at your home for a month (or more) in which you make a special meal; this approach will yield better results than simply attempting a nightly critique of your children's dining etiquette. Keep the experience positive. If you're able, reward your child with a fancy dinner out after a successful dining lesson. Either way, a review of the key points of this chapter is in order before you attempt any very special dining occasions.

8

It's Like, Um, Ya Know, Totally Out of Control

Preventive (or Corrective) Measures
for Unsavory Kid Language and
Other Related Social Phenomena

"For sure, like, totally."
—Valley Girl

In my Intro to Public Relations class at NYU, one of the students began her presentation this way: "The campaign is, like, meant to counter stereotypes surrounding, like, the concept of female beauty, and um, it's meant to, like, empower us, ya know . . . ." I've heard so many students speaking in exactly the same way this young woman did, so I finally decided to challenge my entire class to eradicate the words "like," "um," and "ya know" during presentations—and maybe even from their casual conversation too!

We've all heard them, and almost everyone uses them, but these infectious filler words are grammatically useless and downright distracting—certainly during a presentation before peers in class, let alone in the workplace. I have sometimes found it difficult to focus on the content of a student's presentation because the words were, like, used, like, so often that I, um, couldn't concentrate on, like, anything else. All I could think about was how my students would come across during a job interview.

And that's how this portion of the socialsklz:-) curriculum was born. We even have a sign in the entryway of our classroom that warns, "This is a 'like' 'um' and 'ya know'-free zone. Beware— violators will be issued Frownie cards." The Frownie cards are red, blue, and purple frowning faces corresponding to "like," "um," and "ya know." When students use these junk words, the instructor issues cards to the offenders.

The English language is rich with words for describing our thoughts, actions, and everything else, and yet we use the same ones over and over again, often cluttering our sentences with distracting repetitions and useless fillers. I understand the concern about using "big" words: people might think we're elitist or snobby. The trick is to find a middle ground in which you express your thoughts and feelings by using your vocabulary to the best of your ability. When you speak eloquently, people will much more readily respect what you have to say.

The English language is fluid and evolving: words change, pronunciation and intonation changes, and slang pushes the envelope, requiring us all to adapt. The ubiquity of "like," "um," and "ya know" is just one phenomenon, but the staying power of these filler words has surprised even linguists. I've made it my mission to increase awareness among students, showing them the importance of using a vibrant vocabulary and fewer junk words. Even if they only make these changes in our workshops, it's a start in raising awareness. I taught this lesson in a public school in New York City recently and when I later returned to the school, one of my students told me that when her best friend recounted a story about her weekend, she had used "like" ten times.

I'm not saying that my vocabulary is perfect: I've had to work on my own use of filler words, and once in a while kids at our workshops rightly call me out. But the goal is to address how frequently these words roll off our tongues. When we issue Frownie cards, kids can't believe the frequency with which they use filler words, and they do everything in their power to try to stop themselves. Quite a few students found it impossible to avoid "liking" and "you knowing," so they decided not to speak at all. I even had two tween girls who decided that the only way they were able to avoid "liking" was to, "ya know," speak painfully slowly. Much to their chagrin, they were disqualified even then.

In researching this book, I came across a fascinating study by Russell, Perkins, and Grinnell (2008) that looked at the effects of hiring decisions based on an interviewee's use of "hesitations and discourse markers" such as "like" and "uh." As it turns out, these markers may very well affect how professional a person is perceived to be. "Participants in the study consisted of students between the ages of 18 to 43 years and professionals between the ages of 22 to 76 years. Across the board, both adult professionals and students were less likely to be wanted for hire, were perceived as less professional, and were less likely to be recommended for hiring if they overused the word 'like' compared to 'uh.'"[1] Note that the students themselves, who often fall victim to overusing the word "like," concurred with the adult professionals. Just another reason to help your children eradicate these unnecessary filler words.

In this chapter, we'll have some fun addressing a few of the more irritating linguistic habits and we'll also address questionable social behaviors that are often difficult for a parent to confront without appearing to insult, reprimand, or nag their children. In my workshops, I have the advantage of being a non-parental figure, but I'll show you an effective way to teach these skills in a parental role, so that everyone in the family (not just the children) can benefit. After all, we all have issues we need to work on.

Five Common Unsavory Social Behaviors in Kids

• Using filler words ("like," "um," and "ya know") excessively

• Pointing at others

• Cursing

• Using slang

• Public grooming and hygiene

LESSON

In this chapter, we will address a broad array of linguistic issues and social phenomena that you may have been dying to address but just weren't sure how to. In the past, you may have tried to contend with these issues without success, but this chapter will show you how to do so effectively. It is important to approach these exercises with a light touch, as the lesson can be somewhat sensitive in nature. Because some children may be offended by your attempts to correct them, it's important to be upbeat and nonjudgmental, and to include yourself in the lesson whenever the topic may relate to you too. In workshops, I always share examples from my own life so that no one feels ostracized or singled out. I usually mention a particular bad habit I had when I was 8 years old: I'd constantly scrunch up and wiggle my nose; over time, it became an entirely unconscious habit. My friends would tease me about it and my brother would embarrass me by imitating my habit. The problem was that I didn't know how often I was doing it. To help me break the habit, my mother took it upon herself to clap every time I did it. Although it was irritating when she clapped (thankfully, she only did it in the privacy of our own home), it put an end to my twitch. (I'm not saying that extreme measures are the perfect remedy for any unwanted habit; I share my story only to illustrate a point.)

Let's begin with the "like," "um," and "ya know" craze. I asked the parents of some students about the origins of "like," but it was difficult to pinpoint exactly when the overuse began. Some remembered the song and movie *Valley Girl*. Others believe that "like" as a filler was coined specifically in California (you may have seen "The Californians" on *Saturday Night Live*). Whatever the origins, it has become so ingrained in our speech that it's nearly impossible to eradicate. Remind your kids that "like" is the only word of the three that can actually be used in a grammatically appropriate way.

Ask kids to open their journals and start a new entry called, "It's, like, um, totally out of control, ya know?" Ask them to write a few sentences in which they use "like" correctly. They'll likely (this is an appropriate use of "like"!) come up with sentences such as "I like playing video games," or "I like mint chocolate chip ice cream," to express their approval of something or use the word in the context of "liking" something on Facebook. But there is also another grammatically correct way in which we can use the word "like"—in comparisons. For example, "My dog looks like a human being," or "That smells like vinegar."

After reviewing the correct uses of "like," you can address "um" and "ya know." They actually aren't grammatical: they're just conversation fillers. So, like, now you should, um, take this opportunity to have an energetic, junk-word-filled conversation with your children to highlight the ridiculousness of the phenomenon, ya know? Often the first thing that comes out of many children's mouths when they raise their hands and are called on is, "Um. . ." But you'll surely hear it elsewhere in their language, too.

It is now time to initiate a game during which no one is allowed to use these words as fillers. The duration of the game is up to you—it can last for ten minutes or for the entire lesson. Consider yourself forewarned: kids can become very animated and crafty in avoiding these buzz words, and the game can get rowdy, which might be distracting if it goes on for too long. My students take great delight in calling me out for using the words, even if I am referring to them in context of the game. During this game, you (and only you) will play referee and issue Frownies to the players. If you don't want to make Frownie cards, you can simply list the three junk words in your child's journal and keep a tally. (It's a good idea to minimize the focus on the Frownie cards and instead to keep the focus on the lesson.)

If you're going to use Frownie cards, label a slip of paper with each player's name. Make one for yourself too, as you're part of the game (and you might have to issue yourself a few violations!) This paper will serve as the tally for each player's "like," "um," "ya know" score. At the end of the designated game time, tally the scores. Remember, you are the only one who can issue violations; let kids know that if you don't hear it, it's not a violation! At the end of the game, the player with the fewest violations is the winner.

You can always toss in a specific junk word from your own household. (In the workshop, we added a "pointing" violation as part of the game. Pointing is neither appropriate nor polite, but many players engage in it, especially as the violations add up.) The game will be most effective if you can encourage your children to continue to speak naturally. Ideally, by noticing how many times they use these words during the game, your children will become more aware of how often they use junk words on a daily basis.

Slang

Ask kids what they think "slang" is. It might be a good idea to look up the dictionary definition. Dictionary.com defines *slang* this way: "noun 1. very informal usage in vocabulary and idiom that is characteristically more metaphorical, play-ful, elliptical, vivid, and ephemeral than ordinary language, as *Hit the road*. 2. (in English and some other languages) speech and writing characterized by the use of vulgar and socially taboo vocabulary and idiomatic expressions."

Slang typically sends tremors through the spines of old-school English teachers. Although it has a largely negative connotation, I don't like to couch it as a bad thing necessarily (unless it's used abusively, per the definition). We often chat with friends in a less formal way, as when we're speaking about something familiar. I tell kids that it's okay to be informal with friends. However, there is a time and a place for everything. Using slang with adults, with teachers, or during interviews is not appropriate. Let's go over some of the slang you might hear your kids using. With younger children, who might not yet be using much slang, treat the topic as a preventive measure.

Start another heading in the journal and ask kids to write down any slang they've heard or used recently. If necessary, give an example or two. (Don't worry that you're introducing them to questionable language because you're not—they've heard it already!) Take the simple example of using the word "yeah." Kids use the word when chatting with friends all the time, which is fine, but particularly with adults and authorities it is a good idea to use language that is a bit more formal. "Yes" is much more appropriate and shows respect. The phrase, "What's up?" has entered many young people's lexicons and is also acceptable to use with friends. Review the slang that your children list in their journals (you might add a term or two that you've heard in their social circles) to determine which words are okay to use with friends and which need to be moved into the "junk words" category and put to rest. Take a moment to demonstrate a few examples of more formal ways of speaking. "Wanna go and get ice cream?" could be changed to "Would you like to get an ice cream?" Similarly, rather than saying, "I dunno" in response to a question, one could say, "I wouldn't mind either way. Why don't you decide?" Create a few informal sentences that kids can enter in their journals, and then ask your children to "translate" them into more formal language.

Just as with verbal slang, there is a time and a place for written slang. Sending "IDK," "OMG," or "LOL" via text, abbreviating in emails, starting an instant message with "Hey," or using emoticons are all fine in the right setting and with friends. My decision to spell socialsklz:-) the way I did and to add an emoticon highlights that very point. However, when we write an email to someone we've never met before or to a professor or a teacher, it's appropriate to use a more formal tone. I often hear complaints from people in the workforce about the way in which interns and new hires use language in a casual and informal fashion. Email in a corporate setting should take the form of a written letter, in the way that we laid out for greetings and introductions in Chapter 2 (page 55): formal salutation, opening, body paragraphs, closing, and signature. Signing off with both a first and last name is essential in formal correspondence. This is a great lesson for kids now that will carry into the future.

Lying

I want to address the touchy subject of lying, a very bad social habit. Kids lie for all sorts of reasons, but it's a topic to address and include in an overall toolkit for life. I like to share the following story with my students. When a friend was being interviewed for a job, she was asked about the lead story on the front page of the New York Times. Although she hadn't even seen the paper that day, she responded with, "Yes, what a great story." The interviewer then asked what she thought about the topic more specifically and she turned bright red. She had no idea. Needless to say, she lost the opportunity to work for her dream company. Small lies, big lies, white lies, half truths: steer away from all of them. When we call certain lies "white lies" we encourage children to believe that some lies are benign or acceptable. Addressing difficult matters in life can be tough, but teaching a child how to do so is a crucial skill. For example, if your child is asked to go on a playdate with someone he or she doesn't want to play with, saying "no," kindly, is great practice, not only for the moment, but for life. In declining a playdate, kids sometimes disappoint, upset, or let people down, but the power of "no" is liberating in all senses of the word.

Talk with your children about how to be compassionate when saying no. In the above playdate scenario, it might mean saying more than just "No, I can't." Instead, try "I'm sorry I can't, but thank you for the invitation." There is no need to go into great detail as to why, but a "thank you" offers more compassion. And if your child really did want to go, he or she might say "I'd love to, but I have a something else to do that day. I really appreciate your asking. Maybe another time?" Here is the bottom line: teach your child how to say "no" confidently and honestly because eventually, the truth always comes out. Encouraging your children to say "yes" throughout life when they really mean "no" is a terrible disservice to them.

Swearing and Disrespectful Language

Although these next few topics might potentially fall into the "manners" category (shhhh), let's be proactive and address them. It's best to catch bad habits early—before they become so ingrained that they're nearly impossible to change. If you don't intervene and correct the bad habit, it can become so insidious that it will last an entire lifetime.

I'll just quickly touch upon swearing by saying that it's never appropriate. Most parents will probably agree, but I want to add that it's a disservice to language and intellect, both of which I love sharing with students. Occasionally when I'm walking behind someone on the streets of New York I'll hear the "F bomb" flying out every few words. I have a very smart, lovely friend who throws around expletives so often that they've become her "filler" words. And sadly, the sweet side of her personality winds up coming across as hostile, disrespectful, and well, like a drunken sailor. In our beautiful language, there are myriad ways to express passion, disdain, anger, joy, and excitement, so why use these ugly words, limiting ourselves to such simple vocabulary? Swear words can also leave a very bad impression on others. If your child has a habit of using any of these words, get to the bottom of it now. And even if your kids aren't tempted to use curse words, educate them on how bland these words really are. Consider alternatives for the words and help your child to use those until the unpleasant words can be entirely eradicated. I'm partial to "fudge," "crumb budget," "for Pete's sake," "drat," and "holy toledo;" a woman in our office, Monique, says "holy guacamole," which I love. It takes time, but do it now before your children are already years into the habit. The same thing goes for the middle finger or "flipping the lid." It's never, ever appropriate, not even in jest.

I bet you've heard the infamous "whatever," perhaps accompanied by an eye roll. Have you been "whatever-ed" at any point in the course of your child-rearing? Or has someone rolled their eyes at you? It's quite memorable and disrespectful, and in a social context it can be a major faux pas too. I ask my students to express their disapproval in a specific way rather than settling for the bland "whatever" and walking away. It's another easy out. "Whatever" is akin to sweeping the situation under the rug. In other words, it leaves the matter unaddressed and unacknowledged by either party. Instead, encourage children to tell someone how they feel. Doing so actually feels good and it will teach your children the value of clear communication, which will serve them well throughout their lives.

Grooming and Other Personal Behaviors

Similar to bad and otherwise disrespectful language, some kids (and adults too!) need to be taught that public grooming is a big no-no. Nail biting or clipping your nails, applying makeup, ear cleaning, picking your teeth—all of these belong at home or in a bathroom. Yes, it happens: you're out in public and you get something stuck in your teeth, or realize your nails haven't been cut in some time or your polish has chipped, or you find a hair growing in an unwanted place. Just find a restroom or private place to take care of it—or wait until you get home. Nail-biting is a habit that befalls many of us at some point, but it's gross. No one wants to shake hands with someone who has been biting his or her nails. Although girls might not be applying makeup yet, they may be in the future. You can get away with applying Chapstick, lip balm, or a pale lipstick, but if it requires a mirror, don't do it at the table or in public. Personal grooming is called "personal" for a reason: don't perform these necessities in the presence of others. I've seen people doing all sorts of grooming while they're on the subway, and it's downright nasty! I still haven't figured out why some people think it's acceptable to groom themselves underground, nor do I understand why someone would even invent keychain nail clippers.

At times we simply cannot avoid sneezing or coughing in public. Just make sure you do it gracefully and in such a way that you are considerate of others. Turn away so that no one will be in the line of spraying germs, and if you don't have a tissue at hand, use your elbow. The common-sense thinking is that you're not using your hands, so you reduce the chance of spreading germs. Either way, try to get to a restroom to wash hands soon after. Review with children whether their sneezes are too loud—they can be toned down. And if a cough or sneeze persists, children should step out of the room to avoid spreading germs. In class, I've demonstrated in a fun way just how easily germs can spread. At the end of the lesson, I poured a bit of glitter into my palm and then shook hands with the students as they departed. I then asked them to look at their palms and to take note that germs, just like glitter, spread very easily. It highlights the importance of keeping hands clean.

Although yawning is a natural response to feeling tired, you shouldn't do it in class, while people are talking, or really anywhere in public. If a yawn slips out, use the same technique you'd use when sneezing: turn away and cover your mouth.

One way that we can be kind to others is to let them know if their personal hygiene is out of order: a zipper down, hair awry, toilet paper on a shoe, shirt on backwards, etc. Be sure to speak to the person privately with a helpful, "I just wanted to let you know your zipper is down." In my office we have a pact that we tell each other when anything personal is out of order. No one wants to walk around in an embarrassing state: especially when teaching socialskilz:-)! If your child points out this sort of issue to you or someone else, thank him or her.

One of my favorite topics to discuss with students is gum chewing—probably because I absolutely loathe it. Start by handing out a package of gum to kids. Once they've all begun chewing away, ask them to take a moment, close their eyes, and listen to the sound of their chewing. You might want to add a little humor to the lesson by exaggerating your own chewing—smacking, snapping, blowing bubbles, etc. Gum chewing can be distracting, annoying to others, and even disrespectful. Yet people seem to be chewing gum everywhere these days—in church, at school, at the movies, and recently, I watched a politician chewing gum at a press conference. The key is to figure out with your children whether they're able to chew gum without smacking it, popping it, or showing it. If they can't, then they shouldn't chew gum in public, period. It should be reserved for the privacy of a bedroom because, yes, it can even be bothersome to other family members. Open journals and determine with your children the places in which they can chew gum discreetly, and the places that are wholly off limits. Write down any formal places that come to mind: school, synagogue, doctor's office, or a wedding. These are places where gum chewing is definitely a no-no, and children should be particularly stellar with their socialsklz:-).

Don't forget to address the topic of gum disposal. Once when I was at Caroline's, a comedy club, the performers asked the audience to look under their tables and count how many pieces of gum were there. The entire audience was aghast. I hadn't the faintest idea that tables were such a popular place to park used gum. Gum is to be discarded in the garbage, not on the street. In New York the sidewalks are covered with black spots where people have discarded their used pieces of gum. I ask students to go to the windows and look down, and then I ask if they know what the spots are. When depositing gum in the garbage, either place it in a tissue first or spit it directly in, so that you don't use your fingers. If you do need to use your hands, wash them afterwards. Ask kids to show you how to discard gum properly.

The tone of this chapter is meant to be light-hearted and fun. With that in mind, consider addressing your kids' bad habits during the lesson, in an unthreatening way, instead of intervening at the moment you see them committing the faux pas. Does your child have a bad habit that you want to help him or her work on? And dare I ask, do you?

❦ REVIEW AND PRACTICE ❧

Here's an idea that provides a great review for this lesson. Ask each person to share a story—something simple, such as "What I did last weekend"—without using any filler words or any other unsavory habits they are working on. Once you figure out a topic, everyone in your group, including you, gets up in front of the room to talk for a set amount of time (one minute for the young kids and two minutes for the more advanced). Give kids a few minutes to brainstorm what they'll be talking about and then time their talks. As a group, discuss unsavory behavior you notice in public and then add another heading in the journal: "Things I'm working on." Everyone should have at least three things to be working on. After the speeches, consider offering a small reward to your children for avoiding junk words and bad habits, or for correcting themselves after they let a "like" slip out, for example.

APPLICATION AND GOALS

The idea of this lesson is to send children out into the world to be the best they can be. Because this chapter covers a broad range of topics, you may want to add some issues that are specifically relevant to your own household. As you include new topics, make sure you do so in a constructive setting, emphasizing that each is an important aspect of being a socially well-adjusted human being. Children should understand that a key part of life requires us to continually strive for self-improvement and to be our personal best. Eliminating nasty habits and poor use of language is just one of the ways in which we can do this.

9

The Real World: Introducing Independence

"It's so easy. We all do it from time to time. We love them so much. We just want to protect our children from anything that might harm them. So we reach out our arm and gather them in. We do their chores for them so they can enjoy a few more moments of play. But these choices carry consequences. When you shelter your children or do what they can do for themselves your children become overly dependent. Worse, they don't challenge themselves or develop self-confidence. Learning self-reliance and independence comes early. But it doesn't happen without your help. You need to support your children by teaching them to be independent."[1]

—Dr. Charles Sophy, Child and Adolescent Psychiatrist

Although you've likely spent the majority of parenthood protecting your children from harm by accompanying them to their activities, to school, and to various social functions, this chapter is about instilling independence and competence in your children outside the home. The word "independence" might make you shiver, and the thought of your precious little ones heading out into the world on their own can be daunting. However, one of the cornerstones of successful parenting is preparing your children for life's demands and instilling in them a can-do attitude and a sense of confidence in being on their own. This doesn't mean that they won't need you for love, guidance, and support—they absolutely do—but self-reliant children are better suited to function effectively, especially later on as adults. It's also a tremendously rewarding experience to see your own children flourish as independent beings, and eventually get jobs and live on their own. But we have to guide them to be independent, and it's often an even more difficult task for parents to let go than it is for children themselves.

Independence and self-competence need to be taught consciously; children master these new skills by practicing them in the real world. Children will gain confidence in themselves when you tell them how great they are, but they'll also see their own success and know instinctively that they've done something great on their own. During this portion of our workshop, we take the children on outings, and we take great delight in hearing the compliments they receive. On outings to our local farmers' market, it's not uncommon for our students to get something extra, just because the salesperson is so impressed by their behavior. Since words of praise often mean more when they come from the outside world, make the deliberate effort to allow your child to take steps towards becoming independent in public. They can even gain confidence from their failures as learning experiences by acknowledging and growing from them (more on this in Chapter 10, page 193). But don't make the mistake of assuming your children will be fine on their own just because they've watched you act in the parental role. They still need intentional instruction. As we undertake the various exercises and activities in this chapter, the ultimate goal is for you to provide the lessons, guidance, and know-how to your children so that they can eventually operate efficiently without you and take on the world on their own.

I was compelled to make this lesson part of the socialsklz:-) curriculum because of a phone call I received at New York University. Towards the end of the semester, I received a call from the parent of one of my students. She called me at my office—not my office at NYU, but my own office where I had my PR business. I was dumbfounded and immediately thought the worst, as images of speeding taxis, subways, and armed muggers clouded my vision. Much to my surprise, the parent told me that she wanted to discuss the grade I had assigned the student for a project. I was shocked on so many levels. Since when do the parents of college students call professors about something as simple as a grade? Did my student even know his mom had called me? I took a deep breath to gather my thoughts. What confused me most was that this parent had tracked down my private office number and that she felt comfortable enough to call me there. I politely asked her how she had gotten my contact information, as it was not available through the university, and then I decided to speak the truth.

I began by explaining that college is the last stage before our children enter the "real world," and that kids who don't know how to cope with life's everyday challenges are truly at a disadvantage, especially when they enter the work force. Then I explained how sad it was that she was making the call for her son. I chose to use the word "sad:" by calling me herself she was communicating to her son that he was unable to manage negotiations on his own. As we concluded the call, I suggested that her son approach me after class to discuss the issue at hand, but he never did.

This experience proved to me that kids with "helicopter" parents—parents who hover—often aren't prepared to maneuver in the real world. They might get the best educations, have a long list of volunteer experience, and get excellent SAT scores, but being sent out into the world without the ability to handle confrontation, decision-making, and difficult situations is tremendously detrimental to their ability to participate in our society. Without the skills necessary to co-exist with others in a pro-active, mature, independent way, we can often end up feeling embarrassed and ashamed. Needless to say, for the rest of the semester this particular student did not once look up from his tablet.

The whole experience led me to think hard about the critical skills a parent must bestow on children to enable them to thrive independently. I came to the conclusion that the nuts and bolts of independence include being able to communicate, being considerate of others, and being organized, able to make decisions, aware of physical and mental surroundings, and self-aware. It is the combination of these elements and a few others that comprise the "Be Independent" portion of our socialsklz:-) essential workshop series. It's always a favorite of our students, and almost every child I know wants to learn how to be independent and how to function effectively in a way that makes him or her proud, and parents proud, too.

In the Introduction of this book I mentioned an email I received from a woman with the subject line: "HELP!" She wanted to speak with me about her twenty-something son, who had graduated from college some three years earlier and was still unemployed. As I read, I realized that she and her husband were classic helicopter parents. They had given their son everything that they themselves had not had; once they divorced, they were motivated to do anything to make their son happy. Later, we talked on the phone and she acknowledged that her son did not have the basic social skills to get past a first job interview, let alone get a job interview set up for himself. Her friend had gotten him an interview, but later confided in her that he was "just really awkward" and that he was "way too casual during the interview." If you find that you fall into this style of parenting, step in (or perhaps step out) to be certain your child is prepared to manage life on his or her own. What's more, these lessons will enrich your relationship with your children by allowing them to feel that you trust them to accomplish things on their own.

Five Common Problems that Keep Kids from Functioning as Independent Beings

- **Unable to make decisions quickly**
- **Unaware of others or surroundings**
- **Don't take responsibility for actions**
- **Don't understand the importance of being organized**
- **Don't manage time effectively**

LESSON

By the end of this chapter, students will learn how to act independently in the world in age-appropriate ways. In a public setting, they will interact with cashiers, place orders with ease, be mindful of others, manage time, learn self-control, be responsible, take initiative, and understand why it's important to be organized. The goal for parents here is to teach the lesson and then intervene as little as possible, as you learn to trust your children's autonomy.

This is an especially enjoyable, interactive chapter that culminates in an excursion out on the town. Ask children to open their journals and write what "independence" means to them; they might list specific examples or a more general definition. Ask if they'd like to be independent or to be able to do things on their own now or at some point in the future. Sometimes we have a child or two in our workshops who is frightened by the concept of going out on his or her own. If your child is similarly nervous, let him or her know that it's okay to be a little bit nervous and ask if he or she would eventually like to go out alone or with friends. Reassure your kids that you will be working together toward independence rather than sending them out to fend for themselves. And if your children are already doing some things on their own, ask what they're looking forward to doing independently.

For this lesson, you can keep track of your child's progress by writing about the lessons and activities in their journals. I'll be discussing what we incorporate in our workshops, but you might want to customize the activities based on your location or surroundings, to cater the lesson to what is most relevant to your child.

Being prepared is perhaps the most crucial part of being independent. For the first excursion, select a variety store or convenience store (here in NYC, we usually take the kids to a corner store)—a place where there is a large variety of items to purchase. You want to present your child with the challenge of making a swift and intelligent choice. Once you decide where to go, prepare a large tote bag for each child: you should fill the bag with a variety of items in a disorganized fashion. The idea is that the child has to go through the bag and decide what they need for the excursion, and what can be left behind. I always include things like a scarf, a wallet, cell phone, toys, snacks, keys, water, a newspaper, an umbrella, bracelets, books, a watch, socks, shoes, toys, and other fun, but distracting, items. Begin by asking your child to sort the items into two piles: what they need and what they don't need. Then ask your child to place the items they will need back into the bag in an organized fashion. The point of this exercise is to demonstrate to children that they should be able to easily find an item in the bag, and that means they can only take so much stuff with them on the excursion.

After your child has done the sorting exercise, discuss what is necessary to bring when you venture out of the house and why. Ask kids to add another heading in their journal under "Independence"—call it "Prepared" and list what they'll need for this particular journey, including any items that weren't in the bag. Here is a list of common basics for when we leave home: a phone; a watch to ensure that we're back on time; a wallet with designated places for change, receipts, cash, and credit cards, to pay for what we choose to buy; an umbrella, if it's raining or if it's supposed to rain while we're out; emergency contact card; keys to get back into the house; and any other items specific to your child or your home. For example, if you have allergies, you might need an Epi-pen; if your home or garage has a passcode, you will need that; if it's especially cold, you might need gloves and a hat. Take only what is necessary, so you aren't weighed down with unnecessary items. Finally, give your children a designated amount of money. I suggest starting with a modest amount like $5 or $10 and some loose change for the wallet.

Beat the Clock

Once the bag is organized with the items for their excursion, time your child to see how quickly he or she can locate a specific item. Set the timer (your smartphone should have one), call out the name of an item, and say, "Ready, set, go!" The goal is to locate any item within ten seconds. I always stress the importance of this exercise: it's essential to be able to access your transit card if you're on public transportation, or to easily find the keys to your home. Otherwise, you might miss a subway or a bus, which can make us late, and it's no fun to be outside rummaging through your bag for keys when all you want to do is be home and in your pajamas. Highlight this point in such a way that it is specific to your surroundings and supports the concept of being organized.

Just in Case. . . Emergency Contacts

Create an emergency contact card and laminate it so that kids can always carry it with them. The card should include all the important information, such as parents' names, parents' cell phones, home phone, address, child's allergies or health-related restrictions, and doctor information. Even if your kids know these numbers and your address by heart, in a stressful situation they can forget these vital pieces of information. You can also help your children memorize this information by incorporating a game of flash cards into the lesson, or by creating a jingle with the information in it, because songs can be committed to memory fairly easily. It is remarkable how many kids don't know their home addresses or parents' mobile numbers: make sure your children do. Together with your children, place the card in their going-out bag so that they can easily access it.

Checklist

✓	Greetings	✓	Decision-Making
✓	Outside Social Graces	✓	Time Management
✓	Money Management and Self-Discipline	✓	Pleasantries
		✓	Customer Relations

Now that things are organized, we'll focus this portion of the lesson on the various tasks and social behaviors associated with being "out on the town" as an independent kid. You can check off each one as it's completed.

GREETINGS

Start by thinking through how many people we greet each day when we go out: other passengers in the elevator, doormen, cashiers, or other customers in line. I go to Central Park every day with my daughter and our polite pooch, Mica Girl (you don't have to leash your dog in Central Park as long as it's before 9:00 a.m.). I often say "good morning" or "hello" to other dog walkers. After all, we're all out there together in the early mornings, with our dogs, and some of us see each other regularly. On weekends, my husband joins us; occasionally, he'll keep track of how many responses I get when I say hello to other dog owners. Even though some days I'm only two for twelve, that doesn't mean I stop saying hello! The beauty of friendly greetings is that they are usually welcome, so much so that I now have a network of wonderful people from the park, including a young lady who helps take care of our baby.

You may not live in a major city where you see countless people every time you go out, and you might not have a doorman in your building, but your child will encounter people to whom they can say, "Hello" or "Good Afternoon."

OUTSIDE SOCIAL GRACES

These graces are the ones we use when we open doors, keep to the right on the sidewalk, step out of someone's way, or show respect for passersby who are elderly, pregnant, or disabled. You should also give up your seat on public transportation to any of these people. Children might be confused by the concept of giving up their seat to someone else, since we parents often give up our seats so our kids can be more comfortable. Unless you happen to have a physically disabled child, explain that they're able to stand more comfortably than someone who is much older, someone who is pregnant or carrying a baby, or someone who has a physical disability.

MONEY MANAGEMENT AND SELF-DISCIPLINE

Explain to your children that they are allowed to spend an allotted amount (you should add your purchasing parameters here); whatever they choose to buy cannot exceed the allotment. As an exercise, you might ask your child to find and purchase a specific item in the grocery store. Make sure that they know to factor in tax (or a tip, depending on the situation). While many grocery items aren't taxed, prepared foods are. As they approach the transaction, explain to your children that they should have their wallets open with their money ready, and that they should be sure to get a receipt after they pay. Remembering to get a receipt is important so kids can show parents what they have spent money on. Explain to your kids that they should exercise self-discipline: don't spend money carelessly or complain if they didn't get everything they want.

How to Calculate a Tip

In the U.S. it is standard to leave 15% to 20% of the bill in a restaurant or café. You could ask older children to calculate the exact percentage, but for an easy shortcut, try doubling the tax on the bill: show them where it will be located.

DECISION-MAKING

Discuss with children the importance of being able to make decisions efficiently. Review the procedure for purchasing an item in a store: you need to be able to negotiate the aisles and make a decision quickly (start with a 5- or 10-minute window, depending on the size of the store). Deliberating excessively or dawdling isn't effective, especially when you need to be home on time. Instruct kids to make their decision before they approach the register; if they are in a group, and a joint decision might be challenging, talk about what the group likes and what they are able to purchase, given their funds. Decision-making should be finished by the time they get in line. It's not polite to keep people behind us waiting.

TIME MANAGEMENT

For this exercise, focus on helping your children manage their time when they are purchasing an item in a store. Allot a certain amount of time for your child to purchase the item and after he has done so, ask him to meet you at the front of the store at a designated time (use a cell phone or a watch as a timer).

Punctuality is a perfect example of something that can be taught. It is one of the easiest ways to show respect for others, and to ensure that they don't worry about us. Take a moment to tell your child about a time when you were late. It seems that whenever I'm running late, a host of things go wrong, simply because I'm stressed and not making good decisions, whereas when I'm on time or even early, I'm stress-free and I don't make bad decisions.

PLEASANTRIES

During this exercise, I encourage children to say something pleasant to at least one person you encounter. It could be as simple as saying, "Excuse me" or "Can I help you reach that?" At the very least, let your child know that he or she should say "Thank you" to the cashier. Place this entry on the checklist as well.

CUSTOMER RELATIONS

Next up on our list is the interaction your little customers are responsible for. An independent child must be equipped with the skills to communicate effectively. Start by reviewing (repetition is so important) the first impression lesson from Chapter 1 (page 26). While we don't necessarily shake hands with people we're interacting with at the store, making eye contact, exhibiting good body language, and saying "Hello" are important. In a busy store, we need to communicate loudly and clearly so that we're heard, also remembering to use courtesy words like, "please," "thank you," or "excuse me." Walk through an example of a transaction your child might have at the store.

CUSTOMER: Hello. How are you today?

CASHIER: Hi, good, thanks. [The cashier tallies the bill.] Your total is $4.79.

CUSTOMER: [Hands over cash.] Here you go.

CASHIER: Here's your change. [Hands over change.]

CUSTOMER: Thank you very much. May I get a receipt please?

CASHIER: [Hands over the receipt.] Sure, here you go.

CUSTOMER: Thanks. Have a great day.

After doing a practice run, review the exercise as closely as you can to figure out how it will go. Give your children money and be sure that they turn over the money at the right time—not too early—and that they've made sure it's not crumpled or hard to handle. Check eye contact, and make sure they're calculating the payment accurately and checking their change, too.

It is very important that you remain on the sidelines while you and your children are out together. This is an opportunity for your children to do the work and for you to demonstrate your faith in them. Once they understand that they are capable of accomplishing this trip independently, they are more likely to believe in themselves. Ultimately, this exercise is fodder for a fun lesson review when you get home, and an enjoyable way to guide your children in effectively operating as independent human beings. If they become frustrated, encourage your children not to give up and ask them to refocus and try again. By persevering, kids will learn that they can overcome obstacles.

ᛚᚲ REVIEW AND PRACTICE ᛬ᛞ

On the journey home, whether you're walking or driving, let your child be your own personal GPS: ask them to direct you. If they tell you to make a left and it's really a right, make the left anyway. It's an opportunity to teach them to cope with getting lost or a little bit mixed up about directions. This exercise is also an important lesson in being aware of your surroundings. Kids often have no idea how to get to a place because parents always take them; they don't have to pay close attention to directions, so it's up to you to begin to develop that awareness.

Once you're home, review the checklist over a snack. Ask your children how they think they did. What was easy? What was more difficult? What did they have the most fun doing? Review each task on the checklist and address what they did well and what could use a little bit of work in the future. Ask if they felt confident about going out on the town on their own, and if not, find out what would make them feel more confident.

ᛚᚲ APPLICATION AND GOALS ᛬ᛞ

Discuss a future excursion during which your children might be able to put their skills to use for additional practice. Figure out a regularly occurring excursion (it could be daily, weekly, or even monthly) that your child can take on as a responsibility. For example, buying milk on a weekly basis at the grocery store is a simple task that you might ask them to take on. Ask them to plan out the trip and to pick three tasks to incorporate the first time around (for example, greeting the vendor, getting a receipt, and holding the door for someone), and then add more until your children can complete the checklist independently. Your ultimate goal is to send them into the store on their own; you'll wait outside where you won't be tempted to intervene. You can review the checklist with your child when he or she returns. One she's had some practice, ask your child to make a dinner reservation or to order lunch from a delicatessen counter while you wait by the door. That requires a bit more interaction and preparation, but offers the opportunity for a great lesson.

Once your children become more comfortable with independence, ask them to keep track of time on these excursions, and also challenge them by giving them a set amount of time to complete a task. They are allowed to take more than the designated amount of time if necessary—but only if they call you to let you know they're running late.

10

The "F" Word

*"I've missed more than 9000 shots in my career.
I've lost almost 300 games. Twenty-six times, I've been trusted
to take the game winning shot and missed.
I've failed over and over and over again in my life.
And that is why I succeed."*

—Michael Jordan

"Success" is a word that we hear so often that we sometimes take for granted that we will be successful in our endeavors. From athletes to musicians to scholars to local heroes, we are bombarded with images of "winners" on the front page of the newspaper or the cover of a magazine. Our bumper stickers proclaim, "My Child Is an Honors Student" and we proudly display certificates and trophies in our children's bedrooms, even if all they say is "Participant." Parents are inherently proud of their children and some parents even think their children are prodigies; in either case, we want them to know it.

It seems like every kid is a winner these days; everyone gets a prize, everyone get a trophy, and everyone is the BEST. It's hard to reconcile the difference between the old view that says, "If you don't win, you're the loser," and the more contemporary line of thinking that says, "Everyone is a winner." It is not realistic for everyone to be a winner at whatever they do; encouraging our children to think that they will always be victorious is a failure of our responsibility as parents, as it essentially distorts reality. Not everyone will become the CEO of a company, and after middle school, children don't get medals and trophies just for participating. Winning is the result of hard work, persistence, devotion, and believing in oneself, but sometimes we lose, even after trying our hardest in all those respects. Every child should be equipped to handle failure because it's an inevitable part of life and it can also have a great force in a child's life. In fact, Paul Tough published an article called "What If the Secret to Success Is Failure?" in the *New York Times Magazine*.[1] In *How Children Succeed*, he discusses failure as a part of the success quotient. The lessons that arise from failure are invaluable and help to build character, which is why I have chosen to close with a lesson about failure.

Recently I was at the US Open and was listening to a commentator discussing why one of the players on the court was losing. According to the commentator, when he was very young, the player had been regarded as the "future of American tennis," and so was overhyped by many professionals and constantly told how good he was. He rose quickly on the circuit, believing that his success and his ability to win were a product of his natural talent instead of the result of arduous work on the court, time in the gym, and discipline. He never learned that as he got older he would have to work hard to maintain his talent and to keep moving ahead. His is the quintessential story of someone to whom success came so naturally in his formative years that he never learned about the work that it takes to continue being successful.

Shortly after the US Open, I took on a new intern in our office. I discovered that Jackie had been a collegiate softball player during her time at Ohio Wesleyan University. She shared with me that throughout the childhood stages of her athletic life, she lived with a "fear of failure" on the field: specifically, she was afraid of letting down her coaches, who regularly condemned failure. She attributes a turn in her career and her athletic ability to a coach who taught her to stop being afraid of failure. That coach explained that Jackie would only be letting herself down if she failed, and that softball is a game of mistakes in which the odds are almost always stacked against you. Jackie explained that this freed her thinking, freed her muscles from tensing, and became a motivating factor in allowing her to take her game to the next level. This coach also left Jackie with a thought that stuck, "If you succeed, don't take it for granted, but don't over-celebrate either."

There are so many correlations between this coach's message and our lives: the game of life isn't easy, we don't win every day, and we don't get accolades for everything we do. Much of our hard work is thankless and failure is a reality. Precisely because kids are so programmed to be successful and to win at everything, they're often plagued with anxiety about failing that prevents them from performing at their full potential. Of course, success should be an important part of every child's life. After all, it builds confidence and it reinforces the idea that hard work yields success, but there must be a healthy balance. We adults have a tremendous amount of life experience that we want to pass on to our children, and yet we do everything in our power to carefully guard our children from the "F" word.

As I write this chapter, I've been thinking a lot about the "F" word. I wanted to get to the bottom of why we teach our children what we've learned from our experiences, but we do everything possible to prevent them from ever failing. I think unconditional love blinds us, so we believe it is our duty as parents to protect our kids from feelings of disappointment and sadness that go along with failure. But we fail to look at the whole picture and account for the lessons kids would learn from failing, if we'd let them. It is a gross disservice to send our children into this world without the ability to manage failure or to recognize the growth that often results from failing. This is personal for me. As I think about my own baby, Addy, I am making a pact with myself: though I will try with all my might to protect Addy from failure, I will teach her that failing is inevitable, that it can be rich and rewarding, and that it often makes us grow, learn, strive for the best and become wiser.

We adults should remember that the path to a successful career, for example, is lined with failures. During a commencement speech at Stanford University, Steve Jobs discussed his own failure: "It turned out that getting fired from Apple was the best thing that could have ever happened to me. The heaviness of being successful was replaced by the lightness of being a beginner again, less sure about everything. It freed me to enter one of the most creative periods in my life."[2] Thomas Watson, founder of IBM, said, "Double your rate of failure. That's where you'll find success."[3] When we talk about failure, we can't forget Abe Lincoln: he was unable to get into law school, lost a run for Congress, twice lost runs for the U.S. Senate, and spent 17 years repaying a loan after his own entrepreneurial ambition to open a storefront left him in debt. In spite of these failures, all three of these great men continued to relentlessly pursue success, using what they learned to grow and thrive.

Angela Duckworth, a prominent psychology professor, formerly a high school math teacher, describes an interesting phenomenon. She researched the way that effort correlates with success in children and concluded that when it comes to high achievement, "grit" may be as essential as intelligence. She describes "grit" as "sticking with things over the very long term until you master them." She writes that "the gritty individual approaches achievement as a marathon; his or her advantage is stamina."[4] Sometimes just being innately good at something is not enough, as I highlighted in the case of the famous tennis player. I've been teaching for years, and I have seen time and again that believing you can do something is often the difference between success and failure.

Learning from our mistakes fosters countless lessons, including determination, humility, commitment, patience, and problem-solving. Don't get me wrong: when failure strikes, it strikes deep, it hurts, and it can be demeaning and confidence-deflating. However, it can also teach children to appreciate what they work hard for, and to associate pride with putting forth effort.

This chapter is meant to guide you, the parent, in highlighting the good that comes from failure (as long as your child has expended sufficient effort) and the hard work that making such an effort often entails. Starting now, it will be your job to praise not only your child's successes, but also his or her failures, and to make a conscious effort to praise effort rather than ability. Consider using your own mistakes as examples in order to show that parents can fail too.

Five Common Misunderstandings
Children Often Have About Failure

• We should never, ever fail at anything.

• Failure is always bad.

• The reason to make an effort is to win a prize.

• If you aren't successful, it's not worth doing.

• Fear of failure should be the principle motivating factor.

LESSON

Ask kids to open their journals and write an enormous letter "F" across the page. Ask them to guess what it stands for, and with older kids, let them know that it stands for a word that they are allowed to say. After they get it right, or give up, explain that it stands for "failure" and ask them what the word means to them. This is the part of the lesson in which you can discuss different types of failure and strive to understand how your kids view failure. I encourage you to open up the dialogue and really try to grasp what they consider to be failure and how it makes them feel. Do they feel weary or anxious about failing? Does failure scare them? Do they think they will never fail?

At the top of a new page, ask kids to write down three things they're really good at. Then ask them to make two columns on the page, and to list three things they feel they've failed at in the left column. This might be a very eye-opening and even emotional lesson for you because it's natural to want to shield our children from failure. Encourage kids to open up; you might consider sharing one of the things that you've failed at in life.

Ask kids why they consider the three things they wrote down to be failures. For example, if they think they failed to do well on a test, ask why. Was it the grade they received? Was it that they didn't study hard enough? Should they have asked for more help to understand the material? This exercise is not about making excuses, but rather about owning our failures and taking responsibility for them. Help your kids connect actions with consequences and ask what they think they could have done differently to improve their score. If your child writes down that she failed at being a good friend, inquire as to why and how. In some instances, kids will consider trying hard without succeeding to be a failure, like in the case of trying a new sport. When I was a child, I was athletic and excelled at most sports. But when I gave basketball a try, I quickly realized that I was absolutely terrible. Fortunately, what I learned from that experience was more valuable than being great at basketball could ever have been; I learned to be more patient with people who weren't athletic. I learned to be humble in the sports I did excel at because I understood what it felt like to be the "loser" on the court. I stuck to my commitment to play on the team for an entire season, as painful as it was. I realize now that although I "failed" as a basketball player, I tried out something new, and I realized that in order to succeed, we need to take risks and try new things without any guarantee of being rewarded. If you can think of a similar example in your life, feel free to share it with your children.

Across from each of the three "failures" in the left column, direct your kids' attention to the right-hand column, which can be labeled the "Learned" column. Review what they learned in each of the instances of failure. For example, your child might have learned that he should be more organized and study more efficiently in order to do better on the next test. As for the friendship example, maybe your child learned a lesson about keeping secrets or about not excluding a friend.

Another important aspect of this lesson is to help your children understand exactly what failure is in both their eyes and yours. Direct your children back to their journals to write down a new definition of failure after this discussion. When children cheat, lie, or don't take responsibility for themselves, they fail. If children get caught up in comparing themselves to others, or define themselves by what their friends see, or equate success and material wealth, that too is a failure. Failure can also mean failing to give our best effort, making bad decisions, or being selfish, unkind, or disrespectful in any way.

❧ REVIEW AND PRACTICE ☙

It is important to address what happens when we try our best but don't succeed: this is not necessarily failing, especially if kids learn from the experience. Encourage them to take risks by trying new things, rather than simply avoiding experiences out of fear. As you review this lesson with kids, share with them a story from your own childhood about an activity you hated, but later came to love and excel at. Our strengths and weaknesses are not set in stone; change can happen naturally or it can come as a result of hard work and discipline.

In *New York Family* magazine, Maggie McNamara wrote about her life as a young ballerina. Much to her mother's dismay, after her first few ballet classes, she quit. A few years later, she decided to try hip hop dance and eventually came full-circle back to ballet. This time around, however, she had confidence in herself. She explains, "Every journey has its obstacles, and there were certainly points when I thought I wasn't good enough or that my feet weren't meant for ballet, and so on and so forth. But dance taught me just how stifling those doubts can be and helped me develop the confidence to overcome them."[5]

In a *Wall Street Journal* blog post, Heidi Grant Halvorsam wrote that "When you study achievement for a living, as I do, one of the first things you learn is that measures of 'ability' (like IQ) do a shockingly poor job of predicting future success." She goes on to explain that "It's really about hard work and has very little to do with innate ability."[6] So let's guide our children to work hard and to be persistent. It might even take doing something together to help highlight why persistence is so meaningful.

⚬ APPLICATION AND GOALS ⚬

Make a point this week at dinner to walk through the details of your child's day. Ask about tests, homework assignments, different classes, and extracurricular activities. Then ask how specific activities went and how they make your child feel. If you're asking about an art class, you might say: what projects did you work on this week? How do you think they turned out? Do you think this is a strong suit of yours? Ask your child what she thinks she's good at and what could use improvement. It's great to let kids acknowledge what they're good at themselves; we parents often tell our kids how great they are at a particular activity or in a certain subject even when we know they aren't, so this conversation will shed some light on what they know they are excelling at. And, of course, the exercise is a great way of connecting with kids.

This week encourage your children to try something new that they might not think they're good at. If your child doesn't think he is a good artist, try doing a painting, or if he feels he isn't an athlete, try out a new sport. Once they've tried the activity, ask how they felt they did, whether they'd try it again, and what they learned from it. And as your children experiment with trying something new, give them the opportunity to assess themselves. Listen without judging and if necessary ask a probing question, such as "Tell me what happened," or "What could you do differently next time?" If your child is crippled by the thought of trying something new and failing, try doing the activity together and experiencing failure as a team before asking him or her to do so independently.

For Parents of Children with Special Needs: What This Book Offers You

Shortly after starting socialsklz:-) it was brought to my attention that social skills groups are suggested for children with special needs. Although our workshops are not specifically intended for children with special needs, nor do I have an academic background in that area, I've had a number of parents and guardians who call and ask whether or not we are suited for kids on the spectrum or with other social cognitive deficits.

Last year a mother called and asked to speak with me specifically. She inquired as to whether or not her daughter could attend a workshop and described her child's particular disability. Although initially hesitant, I listened and felt like the program could potentially be beneficial to her daughter and we agreed to give it a try. In the classroom, I quickly saw how useful the socialsklz:-) program was for her, and so did she and her mother. You could see the excitement in this child as she left and a newly developed sense of confidence having learned not only how to make a good first impression, but how she'd connected with the other students in the workshop. Yes, she has particular social delays, but she also saw that other kids have social challenges too. Her mom later mentioned how the program had helped her daughter in her interpersonal relationships both at school and at home, where she'd been suffering from isolation and loneliness. Research suggests that children and youth with disabilities are at higher risk for experiencing lower levels of social-emotional well-being than their peers without disabilities. Taking the time to teach these skills is that much more important with special needs children.

Before children with special needs are enrolled in our workshops, I request a conversation with the parent or guardian to figure out if the program is a fit. And for you at home, before you endeavor upon this book, I suggest that you speak with your child's doctor to gauge how these lessons can be as positive and meaningful as possible. At socialsklz:-) workshops , I ask the parents/guardians to come in before the first class so that the student and I (or their instructor) can get to know each other and reach a comfort level. I explain to the child what the program is all about and what we're going to do. I ask if they have any questions and then discuss my expectations of them during the workshop. I also set up a means by which they can notify me if they feel overwhelmed and need to step out of the classroom at any point during the program. I suggest doing something similar at home with your child. Spend more time helping him or understand what you're going to be working on together, as a team and potentially with other children, and that the lessons are meant to be enjoyed and that they'll help him or her out at school and in relationships in general.

Richard Lavoie, M.A., M.Ed. a former special education teacher and administrator, and author of *It's So Much Work to Be Your Friend: Helping the Child with Learning Disabilities Find Social Success*. The book addresses the direct link between learning disabilities and social skills issues that many children face. Lavoie provides specific strategies for parents, teachers and caregivers about how to assist the child in making and keeping friends. The Library Journal praised the book as "a breakthrough." In it he writes that "nearly every learning challenge has a social component; failing to master social competence can have catastrophic effects." Lavoie argues that "social skills are the ultimate determining factor in a child's future success, happiness, and acceptance." He explains that "The research here is overwhelming. The adult success of the person with learning disabilities is largely dependent upon his social-emotional relationship skills—not his academic skills."[1] There is no question in my mind that teaching these skills is crucially important for children with special needs. I've seen the value that teaching this skill set has in many cases and how repetition and reinforcement at home are even more critical.

Before endeavoring to use this book, take some time to watch your child at play and write down specific social areas that you feel need to be addressed. Then read through the book and highlight which chapters you'll spend more time on. As you embark upon the lessons, be sure to keep the fun element a part of the journey you're about to begin, whether it be the two of you or with a group of kids. And take as much time as needed on the chapters, going through each of the subjects at a manageable pace. Take breaks and stop when it's needed. You know your child best.

As you work through the book, point out the strengths that your child has, and work in more depth on the skills that pose a greater challenge without turning the lesson into a critique. There is a great deal of material we are covering in this guidebook, so I'd suggest that rather than doing a lesson per week, spend two weeks in between lessons, applying the skills in various settings with a good deal of patience and care, while referring back to the lesson and journal on a daily basis. Richard Lavoie writes, "It is important to remember that children with learning problems often require intensive instruction, guidance, and assistance to master social skills."[1]

Whether it takes a few months or a few years to get through, there is no question that social skills lessons pave the way to happiness and a greater sense of self-esteem and I'd say that hands-down, the time investment, whether it be months or years, is well worth it.

Here are few questions I've been asked by parents of children with special needs that might be useful to you:

What accommodations or activities should be included when teaching these lessons at home to children with special needs?

Spend time with your child before taking on the book to explain exactly what you'll be working on together and the specifics of what you'll be covering. Also, explain how each "meeting" or lesson will be structured-with a lesson, a review, goals and applications. Perhaps incorporate a regular snack that will be part of the lesson and looked forward to as part of a routine that accompanies these lessons.

At the beginning of each chapter, explain what the theme is and review the vocabulary that will be part of the lessons for example, "first impressions" or "body language" in chapter one.

The hands-on activities in the book are even more meaningful to your children, so be sure to use them not once, not twice, but as many times is needed. If you come up with your own activities that work well, by all means use them (and feel free to share them with me on Facebook or via email. I love hearing about activities that others have come up with!)

Remember, take the time you need without getting frustrated if lessons don't go as quickly as you intend. The beauty of using this book at home is that the lessons can be done at your own pace. If you sense frustration, stop and start the lesson over at a better time. At the end of each lesson, provide an in-depth review of the material covered and then talk in detail about how you'll be apply the material to the week ahead. If need be, review the journal over dinner each night as a refresher.

Will my child feel comfortable working on the same material with children without special needs?

If you're working with other children, your child with special needs may need an extra hand, but should generally be treated as an equal and be encouraged to take responsibility for his or her own work and behavior. In her book *Language, Literacy and Children with Special Needs*, Sally M. Rogow emphasizes the point that "peers without disabilities learn from children with disabilities as the children with special needs are learning from them."[2] Rogow's pragmatic position is that inclusion benefits all children. Author and nationally recognized child and adolescent psychologist Dr. Jennifer Hartstein explains that in some instances other impaired children can bring a child with special needs down, rather than up. She also explains that often times special needs children will rise to the occasion. As I mentioned earlier, I suggest speaking with your child's doctor about what's best.

Should lessons be presented in a different order?

You can move material within lessons around. For example, you might want to kick off a lesson where a child's gifts rather than their weaknesses lie, so that positivity is the starting point and so that frustration doesn't immediately set in. However, I wouldn't suggest moving chapters themselves around because there is a flow to the book and there is material that we refer back to and incorporate into lessons.

Emotional literacy can be difficult for children with special needs to grasp. Is there a method used to help students to read others' emotional states?

Take a bit more time particularly with chapter 3 where I delve into conversation skills. Here in addition to the material covered on starting, maintaining and closing conversations, model different conversational scenarios to encourage children to focus on how to read body language and how others feel and how to adapt to those scenarios .

Notes

INTRODUCTION

[1] Tara Parker-Pope, "School Curriculum Falls Short on Bigger Lessons," *New York Times Blogs: Well*, September 5, 2011, http://well.blogs.nytimes.com/2011/09/05/school-curriculum-falls-short-on-bigger-lessons/.

[2] Perri Klass, "Making Room for Miss Manners Is a Parenting Basic," *New York Times*, January 13, 2009.

[3] see note 1 above.

[4] J.A. Durlak et al., "The Impact of Enhancing Students' Social and Emotional Learning: A Meta-Analysis of School-Based Universal Inventions," *Child Development* 82 (2011): 405-432.

[5] Paul Tough, *How Children Succeed* (Boston: Houghton Mifflin Harcourt, 2012).

[6] Helen Kramer. Interview by Faye de Muyshondt. New York, New York, October 2012.

[7] Allison Rizzolo, "Land of the Rude: Americans in New Survey Say Lack of Respect Is Getting Worse," *Public Agenda*, April 3, 2002, http://www.publicagendaarchives.org/press-releases/land-rude-americans-new-survey-say-lack-respect-getting-worse.

[8] Christine Pearson, "Use of Tech Devices Harm Workplace Relationships," *New York Times*, May 18, 2010.

[9] Amanda Lenhart et al., "Teens and Mobile Phones." *Pew Internet and American Life Project*, April 20, 2010, http://www.pewinternet.org/Reports/2010/Teens-and-Mobile-Phones/Summary-of-findings.aspx.

CHAPTER 1

[1] Carol Kinsey Goman, "Seven Seconds to Make a First Impression," *Forbes*, February 13, 2011, http://www.forbes.com/sites/carolkinseygoman/2011/02/13/seven-seconds-to-make-a-first-impression/.

[2] Chad Boutin, "Snap judgments decide a face's character, psychologist finds," *News at Princeton*, August 22, 2006, http://www.princeton.edu/main/news/archive/S15/62/69K40/index.xml.

[3] Daniel J. Siegel and Tina Payne Bryson, *The Whole-Brain Child: 12 Revolutionary Strategies to Nurture Your Child's Developing Mind* (New York: Bantam, 2012), 33.

CHAPTER 2

[1] Jeffrey Rosen, "The Web Means the End of Forgetting," New York Times, July 21, 2010.

[2] See note 1 above

[3] See note 1 above.

[4] Nick Bilton, "Erasing the Digital Past," *New York Times*, April 1, 2011.

[5] Ulla Foehr et al., "Generation M 2: Media in the Lives of 8-to 18-Year-Olds," *A Kaiser Family Foundation Study*, January, 2010.

[6] Steve Carell, "Princeton University's 2012 Class Day Remarks," *News at Princeton*, June 4, 2012, http://www.princeton.edu/main/news/archive/S33/88/33K92/.

CHAPTER 3

[1] Debra Fine, *The Fine Art of Small Talk* (New York: Hyperion, 2005).

[2] Courtney Fox, "Teaching Children How to Converse," *Responsive Classroom Newsletter*, November, 2011, http://www.responsiveclassroom.org/article/teaching-children-how-con-verse.

[3] Peter V. Handal, "Dale Carnegie Wins Friends in a Digital Age," *CBS Sunday Morning*, January 15, 2012.

[4] Katie Couric, *The Best Advice I Ever Got: Lessons from Extraordinary Lives* (New York: Random House, 2012).

CHAPTER 6

[1] Randy Pausch, *The Last Lecture: Really Achieving Your Childhood Dreams* (New York: Hyperion, 2008).

[2] R. A. Emmons and M. E. McCullough, "Counting Blessings Versus Burdens: An Experimental Investigation of Gratitude and Subjective Well-Being in Daily Life." *Journal of Personality and Social Psychology*, 84 (2003): 377-389.

[3] Jeffrey J. Froh et al., "Counting blessings in early adolescents: An experimental study of gratitude and subjective well-being," *Journal of School Psychology 46* (2008): 213-233.

[4] See note 2 above.

CHAPTER 7
1 Brad Prescott, "The History of Toasting," *Into Wine*, http://www.intowine.com.

CHAPTER 8
1 Russell B. et al., "Interviewees' Overuse of the Word 'like' and Hesitations: Effects in Simulated Hiring Decisions," *Psychological Reports* 102 (2008): 111-118.

CHAPTER 9
1 Dr. Charles Sophy, "Teaching Independence: Developing Confidence and Self-Reliance in Your Child," *SelfGrowth.com*, November 27, 2006, http://www.selfgrowth.com/articles/Sophy17.html.

CHAPTER 10
1 Paul Tough, "What If the Secret to Success Is Failure?" *New York Times*, Sept. 14, 2011.

2 Steve Jobs, "Stay Hungry, Stay Foolish" (speech delivered at Stanford University, 2005). DNA: *Daily News and Analysis* (blog), Oct. 6, 2011. http://www.dnaindia.com/.

3 Matthew Toren, "To Be Successful, You Must Know Failure—Thomas Watson." *Young Entrepreneur*, April 21, 2009. http://www.youngentrepreneur.com.

4 Emily Hanford, "Angela Duckworth and the Research on "Grit." American Radio Works. http://www.americanradioworks.publicradio.org. (Accessed Oct. 2012)

5 Maggie McNamara, "I Hated Ballet—And Now I Can't Imagine Life Without It," *New York Family Magazine* Oct. 1, 2012. http://www.newyorkfamily.com.

6 Heidi Grant Halvorson, "The Success Myth." *At Work* (blog). *Wall Street Journal*. July 24, 2012. http://www.blogs.wsj.com/atwork.

SPECIAL NEEDS SECTION
1 Richard Lavoie. *It's So Much Work to Be Your Friend: Helping the Child with Learning Disabilities Find Social Success*. New York: Touchstone, 2006.

2 Sally M. Rogow, *Language, Literacy, and Children with Special Needs*. Toronto: Pippin, 1997

Bibliography

Candler, Laura. "Teaching Social Skills." Teaching Resources, May2, 2013
http://www.lauracandler.com/strategies/socialskills.php

Carnegie, Dale. *How to Win Friends and Influence People*. New York: Simon and Schuster, 1981.

Couric, Katie. *The Best Advice I Ever Got: Lessons from Extraordinary Lives*. New York: Random House, 2011, 112-114.

Chua, Amy. *Battle Hymn of the Tiger Mother*. New York: Penguin, 2011.

Lavoie, Richard. *It's So Much Work to Be Your Friend: Helping the Child with Learning Disabilities Find Social Success*. New York: Touchstone, 2006.

McGuirk, Leslie, and Alex von Bidder. *Wiggens Learns His Manners at the Four Seasons Restaurant*. Somerville, MA: Candlewick Press, 2009.

Mayer-Schönberger , Viktor. *Delete: The Virtue of Forgetting in the Digital Age*. Princeton, NJ: Princeton University Press, 2011.

Pausch, Randy. *The Last Lecture: Really Achieving Your Childhood Dreams*. Hyperion, 2008.

Siegel, Daniel J., and Tina Payne Bryson. *The Whole-Brain Child: 12 Revolutionary Strategies to Nurture Your Child's Developing Mind*. New York: Bantam, 2012.

Tough, Paul. *How Children Succeed: Grit, Curiosity and the Hidden Power of Character*. New York: Houghton Mifflin Harcourt, 2012.

Notes

Notes

Notes

Notes

Notes

Notes

Notes

Notes

Notes

Notes

Notes

Notes

Notes